Exploring

explOratorium®

KITCHEN SCIENCE

Exploring

explOratorium®

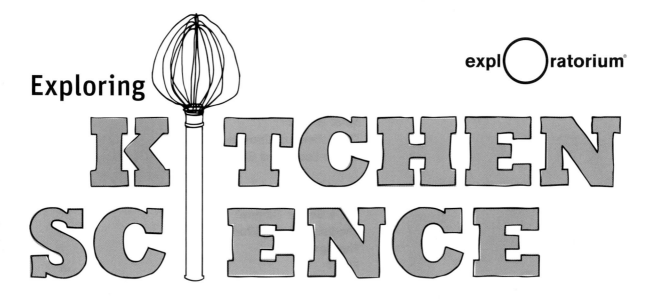

KITCHEN
SCIENCE

30+ Edible Experiments & Kitchen Activities

weldon**owen**

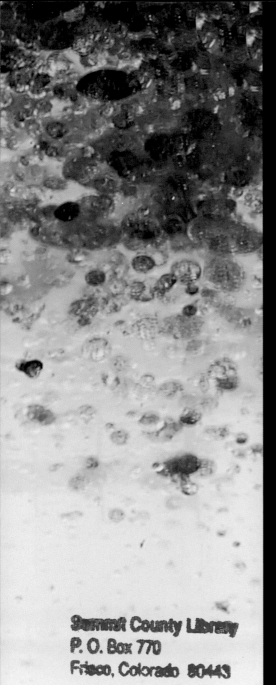

Contents

How to Use This Book

On every plate is a science lesson—a story about where food comes from, how we prepare it, and what it does once we've swallowed it down the hatch! At the Exploratorium, we observe and investigate the full spectrum of science every day, from physics to chemistry, biology to human behavior. Some of our most popular investigations are kitchen experiments using ingredients we eat all the time.

To best learn about the science of cooking and food, we've selected some of our favorite activities that Exploratorium teachers, scientists, and artists have developed over the years. Here's how they work:

YOU'LL NEED

Everything you need to do an activity is listed inside these circles.

THE STEPS

For every activity, there are step-by-step instructions and diagrams to help you make the science happen. But we encourage you to tweak these experiments to explore what interests you—each one is just a starting point for your own personal discoveries.

WHAT'S THE DEAL?

These circles give you the lowdown on the facts behind the fun, explaining all the physical laws and weird science underlying the book's activities.

TRY THIS NEXT!

Sometimes one thing leads to another. For some activities, we've provided fun ideas for further investigations.

INGREDIENTS DEMYSTIFIED!

We've also included profiles on key ingredients that you eat or drink every single day—water, spices, salt, sugar, dairy, and fruit.

Tool Kit

Everyday things—most of which are probably lying around your home right now—will help you do the activities in this book. A few projects require some basic electronics; for those, you can make a quick trip to a hobbyist shop or visit an online retailer. Assemble the tools for each activity so they'll be right there when you need them.

Safety goggles

Safety gloves

Magnifying glass

Syringe

Eggs

Rags and an apron for messes

Pencil and paper

Various glass jars and bottles

Thermometer

Food coloring

Trays and cutting boards

Measuring cups and spoons

Basic baking ingredients (sugar, flour, cornstarch)

Spices

Skewers and toothpicks

FLOUR

A Word for Parents

The activities in this book are designed for kids eight and older. The Exploratorium and the publisher have made every effort to ensure that the information and instructions included here are accurate, reliable, and mind-blowingly cool, but keep your own child's skills and attention span in mind before allowing him or her to try them, and provide supervision as needed. We disclaim all liability for any unintended, unforeseen, or improper application of the suggestions in this book, as well as any stained T-shirts or messy exploding marshmallows. But we're happy to help contribute to your kid's ever-increasing curiosity, of course!

About the Exploratorium

Since Frank Oppenheimer opened the Exploratorium in 1969, we've been an interactive learning lab—a hands-on, playful place to discover and to tinker—and our thought-provoking exhibits and programs have ignited curiosity and delighted visitors far and wide. At our home at Pier 15 on San Francisco's Embarcadero, we host more than 600 exhibits, where visitors can dance with their shadows; build art-making machines; play with magnets, pendulums, and pulleys; and watch the ever-shifting sands and tides of the bay. Come and join us next time you're in the San Francisco area, or visit us at www.exploratorium.edu.

Food
Science
Basics

What Is Food?

Let's zoom in on mealtime to see what nutrition is really all about.

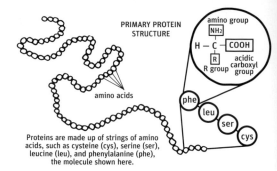

PRIMARY PROTEIN STRUCTURE

amino acids

amino group

NH2

H — C — COOH

R

R group

acidic carboxyl group

phe
leu
ser
cys

Proteins are made up of strings of amino acids, such as cysteine (cys), serine (ser), leucine (leu), and phenylalanine (phe), the molecule shown here.

We eat every day, but do you ever pause to consider what's actually on your plate? In general, food is any substance that creatures scarf down in order to provide their bodies with nutrition and energy. It comes from two main sources: plants and animals. Food from plants takes the form of vegetables, fruits, and seeds, while we eat the meat, milk, and eggs of animals.

When we take a closer look at food, we see that we can break these two groups down further. Food from plants is usually rich in *carbohydrates*, which fuel the body with the sugar it needs to do its thing! Carbohydrates are composed of the elements carbon, hydrogen, and oxygen. Your body easily and quickly digests *simple carbs*, such as the fructose and sucrose found in candy, fruit, or milk. C*omplex carbs*, also called *starches*, such as bread, crackers, and pasta, take more time to digest, and the energy that you get from them lasts longer.

Food derived from animals is commonly rich in *protein*. This crucial stuff helps your body build and maintain itself—it's what your muscles, organs, bones, skin, and immune system are all made of. Proteins are strings of *amino acids*, molecules of hydrogen, carbon, oxygen, and nitrogen (plus a bit of the mineral sulfur). There are twenty amino acids, but your body only makes fourteen—so it needs to get the rest from food to keep itself in good working order.

Next up are fats. Also called *lipids*, fats are made of carbon, hydrogen, and oxygen, too. But lipid molecules have lots more hydrogen atoms. Fats stretch out in long chains, linked by carbon atoms with hydrogen atoms dangling off each. You may have heard that fats aren't good for you, but their bonds provide energy that your body can use when it's low on fuel. We get fats from animals but also from veggies and nuts.

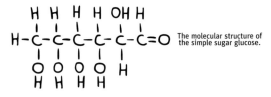

The molecular structure of the simple sugar glucose.

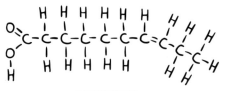

UNSATURATED FAT

You've surely heard a grown-up say, "Eat your vitamins!" Our food is packed with these special substances, each of which performs specific jobs—for instance, the vitamin C in citrus staves off colds, while a carrot's vitamin A aids vision. Our bodies also require *minerals*—dietary elements such as calcium, sodium, potassium, phosphorous, chloride, and magnesium. These assist in transmitting nerve impulses, growing strong teeth, keeping a steady heartbeat, and more.

So there's all this good stuff lurking in your food. How do you know just what's in your sandwich, soup, or bag of chips? Look to the nutrition labels on packaged foods. You'll first see the recommended *serving size*: how much you should eat of that food at one time. All the information that follows is based on that serving size, including how many *calories* (the energy needed to raise the temperature of 1 gram of water by 1 degree Celsius) it contains. There will also be a list of how much a single serving size contributes to the recommended daily intake of fats, carbohydrates, proteins, and relevant vitamins and minerals. Look for a list of ingredients—if an ingredient appears first on the list, the food contains a lot of it!

The Science of Cooking

So you've got food—delicious raw ingredients such as crisp lettuce or fresh tuna. How do they become a meal?

A lot goes into transforming distinct foods into happily harmonized dishes—and each step and method has science at work!

1 Get the right ratios. The first task any recipe requires is preparing your ingredients. This can include measuring liquids or solids (such as cooking oil or sugar) or chopping veggies or fruits. That's because your kitchen is a laboratory, and, as with any chemistry experiment, the materials you use will interact best in certain ratios. Chemical reactions go more quickly when you chop up food to equal sizes, which increases its *surface area* (the amount of exposed tissue) so that it can make more contact with heat, and hence cook at a more consistent rate.

2 Put it together. Often, the next step in cooking is to make a *mixture*: a combination of two or more ingredients in which each keeps its chemical properties. A mixture can be a salad or cookie batter. A *solution* is a type of mixture in which one ingredient is distributed throughout another—much like when you dissolve sugar in water. We create mixtures and solutions because those ingredients will undergo the same chemical reactions together in the next cooking steps.

3 Turn on the gas! When we apply heat to food, we change its chemistry. In the case of boiling an egg, for example, we *denature* its proteins: The heat makes the coils of nucleic acids unwind and bond into solids. The same thing happens when meat hardens and becomes opaque, and when milk solidifies. Similarly, when we heat up a carbohydrate—such as muffins in the oven—they sweeten and brown in a process called *caramelization*. Carbs also soak up water and expand—think of boiling a big pot of spaghetti!

4 Pick a type of heat. Usually, we're cooking with *conduction*: transferring heat to a food through contact. Think of your stove—the flame touches a frying pan, spreading to the oil on the pan and then to the greens you're cooking up. There's also *convection*, in which a moving part (such as a fan or stirring spoon) helps circulate the heat so it warms the food more quickly.

5 Choose dry or moist. Cooking heat also falls into one of two categories: *dry heat* or *moist heat*. Dry-heat methods—such as baking, roasting, and grilling—are very hot (at least 300°F/150°C) and involve zero moisture, creating a crispier dish with more caramelization through a process known as the *Maillard reaction*. Moist-heat methods—such as poaching, stewing, and boiling—use a lower temperature (around 140°F/60°C) and require stock, steam, or another source of moisture. The results tend to be juicier and emphasize the food's natural taste.

Where Does Food Go?

Once we've satisfied our craving, what does our food do for us?

When you chow down on your morning cereal or polish off a slice of pizza, you send your meal on a great adventure through your digestive system. Starting in your mouth, your teeth chew up your food, and then your saliva's *enzymes* (special proteins that help in chemical reactions) soften it. Once the food is easy to swallow, those morsels cruise on down your *esophagus*, a tube that connects your throat to your stomach.

Your stomach breaks down your food even more, using its strong muscles and enzyme-rich juices to churn your snack into a soupy mix. Once properly mushified, this substance flows into the small intestine, a coiled tube that, if it were unstretched, would be a whopping 22 feet (6.7 m) long! Here, food becomes a liquid, and the walls of the small intestine begin absorbing all the nutrients, sugars, proteins, and fats into your bloodstream. The pancreas and liver aid in this process by sending in juices that help break down proteins and fats.

Once the good stuff has been squeezed out of your food and passed into your bloodstream, the blood carries it to your liver for further processing, and then it goes all over your body—transporting simple sugar (glucose) for energy, protein for growth, and nutrients for all sorts of important tasks.

Glucose can't make it into your cells all on its own, however. It needs help from a special hormone, called insulin. (Some people who have problems with insulin are *diabetic*.) Your pancreas creates insulin and releases it when it discovers that your blood has a lot of glucose in it. Insulin then travels to your cells and acts much like a key in a lock, telling the cells to open up and let the glucose in! The cells convert the glucose to energy via a process called *cellular respiration*, breaking the glucose down into carbon dioxide and water, and then storing the energy for all its busy cell activities.

But what about the leftover liquid in the small intestine? It goes to the large intestine, which absorbs any water and lingering minerals that may be of use to the body until there's nothing left but—you guessed it—poop!

Kitchen
Experiments

1. Gustatory hairs mingle with a mix of food molecules and saliva.

TASTE BUD

2. The hairs report what they taste to the taste bud's 50 gustatory receptor cells.

3. The receptors send messages to your sensory cortex via the cranial nerves, and then your brain says, "Yum" or "Ick!"

Try This Next!

Ever tried enjoying a snack when you've got a dry tongue? Go ahead, pat down your tongue with a paper towel. When it's good and parched, close your eyes and have a friend put a bit of cookie or pretzel on it. Can you taste anything? The answer is probably no. That's because you need a liquid medium in order for flavors to bind to the receptor molecules in your taste buds. Thank goodness for spit!

What's the Deal?

On average, the tiny pink bumps on your tongue—called *papillae*—each hold around 15 taste buds. The more you've got, the more you taste. Supertasters have more than 30 papillae in the reinforcement-circle area. They often love sweets but hate bitter things, such as coffee. About half of us have only 10 to 30 papillae in the area. We're just called tasters (yawn). And the rest—"nontasters" who detect flavor but aren't picky—sport fewer than 10. Ask your family members if they like bitter foods. Do the supertasters say no?

1 **Write down everyone's name.** Then ask your first volunteer to dry his tongue with a paper towel.

2 **Drip blue food coloring** on a cotton swab and paint the tip of his tongue. Tell him to swish saliva around and swallow until his whole tongue is beautifully blue.

3 **Stick a reinforcement circle** on his tongue tip. Ask someone to hold the flashlight while you use a magnifying glass to look at your tongue in that circle. Pretty pink bumps—the papillae, which hold taste buds—show up against the blue.

4 **Count** up the papillae you see. Write that number by his name. Now call up the next volunteer and repeat.

Got a Genius Tongue?

Some people don't just taste—they *supertaste*.

You'll need:

Everybody in the house!

Pencil and paper

Paper towels

Blue food coloring

Cotton swabs

Binder reinforcements (the circles you stick around binder-paper holes)

Flashlight

Magnifying glass

Cookie or pretzel

What's the Deal?

You've just learned something amazing: Your nose has a secret superpower. It "tastes" more flavor than your tongue does. In fact, its smell receptors can detect more than 10,000 smells (compared to the only five different kinds of tastes your taste buds can recognize). Your partner probably couldn't accurately guess the juice flavor with her eyes or tongue alone, but her nose knew the real score!

1 **Send your partner** out of the room. Stick a piece of masking tape on the bottom of each glass and number them 1 to 4, making sure she won't be able to see the numbers. Pour one type of juice into each glass.

2 **Drip a different food coloring** into each glass and stir so your partner won't recognize the juice by color alone. Record the number, juice type, and color in each glass on paper.

3 **Call your partner back.** Tell her to hold her nose, sip from each glass, and guess the juice type. If she's like most people, she'll be kind of confused—her eyes and tongue will give her two conflicting flavor messages.

4 **Ask her to let go** of her nose, close her eyes, and sniff the juice before drinking it. Her guesses should be on target now. All hail the mighty schnoz!

The Juice-Tasting Challenge

You taste with your mouth . . . and your nose and eyes!

You'll need:

A partner (a brother or sister will do)

Masking tape

4 glasses

4 flavors of juice

4 food colorings in different hues

Pen and paper

The Agar Lab

Bring molecular gastronomy into the kitchen with crazy noodles and caviar made of fruits and veggies.

① First, let's make noodles out of fruits or veggies using a process called *extrusion*. Roughly chop 1 cup of your fruit or veggies into chunks, put them in the blender and cover with water, and blend until the mix is smooth. (If you want noodles in two different colors, like the golden beet and cranberry noodles pictured here, you'll have to make two batches.)

② Add water so you have 1½ cups (355 mL) solution. Pour it into a pot and bring it to a boil. Once it's boiling, add 0.2 ounces (6 g) of agar powder. Let the mixture boil until the agar completely dissolves, then place a drop onto a plate and watch to see if it gels. If not, add more agar.

③ Time to get squeezing! Affix your tubing to the syringe and push the plunger all the way in, and then draw a small amount of air into the tube. Then place the tube's open end into the mixture and draw brightly colored fruit-and-agar juice into the tube until it's full.

④ Next up, let the tubing cool in a bowl of ice water for 3 minutes. You can leave the syringe attached. Be patient—let the tubing get really cold!

⑤ It's jelly spaghetti trapped in a plastic tube . . . time to get it out! After the jelly has cooled in the tubes, push air into the tube with the syringe and watch the jelly squeeze out in a coil. (It may take a few tries to get it all out.) Arrange on a plate and enjoy!

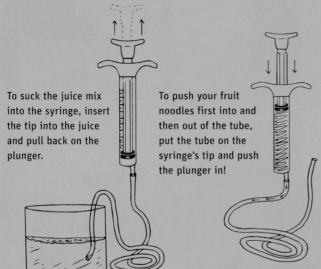

To suck the juice mix into the syringe, insert the tip into the juice and pull back on the plunger.

To push your fruit noodles first into and then out of the tube, put the tube on the syringe's tip and push the plunger in!

Turn the page ⟹

You'll need:

Knife

1 cup (150 g) golden beets*

1 cup (100 g) fresh cranberries*

⅔ cup (160 mL) water

Blender

0.2 ounces (6 g) agar (sometimes called agar-agar)**

Syringe (10–50 mL)

Length of PVC or silicone tubing about 2 feet (60 cm) in length, with a diameter of 2 mm

Bowl of really cold ice water

Jar of canola oil or light olive oil, refrigerated

Eyedropper

Fine-mesh sieve

*These activities will work with any fruit or veggie.
**Agar can be found at online specialty retailers and health- and Asian-food stores.

6 **For the caviar,** you'll use the same agar-fruit mix, but this time you'll put it through a process that molecular gastronomists call *spherification*—a fun way to make food look like little jelly globes. To do so, grab a jar of canola or light olive oil from the refrigerator; it should be quite cold. Take off the lid.

7 **Using the eyedropper,** slurp up some of the juice-agar solution and then drop it slowly into the oil. Watch the solution freeze into little globules as it sinks.

8 **Keep letting drops fall** from the eyedropper until the bottom of the jar is covered in the tiny spheres. Transfer them to a fine-mesh sieve and rinse with warm (not hot!) water. Use your fruit caviar as a mad scientist–style garnish on your next dessert.

What's the Deal?

What's this agar stuff? It's a gelling agent found in dried seaweed (different from gelatin, which is made from animal byproducts). Agar has five times the setting power of gelatin, so you don't need a lot to create shapes that last. Agar melts at 185°F (85°C), but solidifies at 104°F (40°C)—a phenomenon known as *hysteresis*. This means that, once you have your solid agar blobs, you can rinse them in warm water without melting them away. The agar's power is affected by the acidity and sugar content of the liquid with which you mix it. A low pH (an acidic liquid) produces a more weakly gelled product, while a high pH (a sweet liquid) makes a strongly gelled substance.

Fruit

Before you get your morning fruit into your tummy, get your fingers into the fruit to explore the wild varieties of fruit peels, pulp, juice, and seeds. Can't find these exotics in the store? Squish and squash oranges, blueberries, or other available stuff to explore the various ways that fruits carry their seeds.

Noni

Some fruits are protected by cactusy thorns, tough skin, and ultra-tangy flesh—such as noni from Southeast Asia and prickly pears from Central America. Don't be scared: Just peel these guys, slice 'em in half, and chew 'em—seeds and all. Pucker up!

Passion fruit

Passion fruit hails from South America, while the pomegranate is a Mediterranean treat. Both hold their crunchy seeds and sweet juice in panels of tiny sacs called *arils*. Halve the fruits, bang the halves on a bowl edge, and then spoon out and munch the gemlike little arils.

Pomegranate

Prickly pear

Mangosteen

Durian

These fruits hide their bizarre insides behind spiny skin. Thailand's famous durian fruit has big, yolklike pods of sweet but rank-smelling flesh. Rambutan from Malaysia boasts a huge, eyeball-shaped central seed and a layer of flesh that you can nibble away from it.

Giant seeds and teeny seeds: Fruit flaunts both styles. Mangosteen (native to Indonesia) has giant white seeds that you fork out to eat and bitter pulp that you toss. The dragon fruit of Asia and the Americas has zillions of seeds peppered through it. Run a spoon around the flesh to free it from the scaly rind.

Rambutan

Dragon fruit

The Great Egg Conundrum

These two eggs might look the same, but one is cooked and one is raw. Give them a spin to discover which is which!

1 Have a friend place the two eggs on the kitchen table and mix them up while you look the other way. (Hey, no peeking!) Then give both eggs a good spin.

2 Once you get them twirling and whirling, stop both eggs with your hands and then let them go. One will mysteriously spring back into a spin; can you determine which egg it is? Think about it, carefully considering what a liquid interior and a solid interior could do to the egg's motions. Then write down your choice on a piece of paper.

3 Now put this egg aside and turn your attention to the other one. Get it turning very, very fast. Once it's going swiftly enough (at least ten revolutions per second), it might do something crazy: Without any help from you, this egg will suddenly and spontaneously rise up on end and spin like a top. Again, give it a good think—is the cooked egg the stand-up-and-go spinner, or is it the raw egg?

Try This Next!

The egg tricks continue: Grab your raw egg and some table salt. Make a small pile of salt on a flat surface, and then place the egg on the pile with its longer axis pointed up. Gently rock the egg back and forth until it feels stable in its upright position and then . . . let go. Your egg should remain standing! Carefully blow the extra salt away from the egg's base as it stays perched upright on a point below its *center of gravity*: the point inside the egg where it balances left and right, top and bottom, and backward and forward.

What's the Deal?

Drumroll, please: The egg that resumed its spin after being stopped is the raw egg! Inside its shell, the liquid is still spinning, and this motion makes the entire egg go around again. Meanwhile, the hard-boiled egg stands on end because friction destabilizes its spin and causes it to shift position, or stand up. Horizontal frictional forces between the egg and the table nudge the egg so that it spins around its longer axis.

1 **Stick a raw egg** in a cup, and then pour in enough white vinegar to completely cover it. See teeny bubbles forming on the shell? That's carbon dioxide (CO_2), created when acidic vinegar hits the shell's calcium carbonate.

2 **Cover the cup** with plastic wrap and leave it alone for 24 hours. The next day, ladle out the egg with a spoon. See how the shell is dissolving away? Dump out the old vinegar and cover the squishy egg with fresh vinegar. Then put plastic wrap over the cup and let it sit for another 24 hours.

3 **On the third day,** carefully spoon out the egg and rinse it under the tap. The shell should be totally gone now, revealing your naked egg—just an alien-looking blob of white and yolk, held inside a thin opaque membrane.

What's the Deal?

Why does an egg's shell dissolve when you submerge it in vinegar? Vinegar contains acetic acid, which breaks apart the shell's solid calcium-carbonate molecules into their separate calcium and carbonate parts. The calcium ions float free, while the carbonate reacts to make carbon dioxide—the bubbles that you saw forming on the shell when you first dunked it. Be careful with your egg in this form; although it feels like a ball, it will break (not bounce) if you throw it. The egg's yolk is a single cell with a membrane and a nucleus. Do you spot a small white dot on the yolk? That's the cell's nucleus!

Try This Next!

Soak the naked egg in a cup of water overnight. It will swell up, showing you a neat thing called *osmosis*: Because there is a higher concentration of water in the cup than in the egg, water will seep across the egg's membrane to "dilute" the inside and establish equilibrium. Next, try plopping the egg in a cup of corn syrup (made of water and sugar). Now the concentration of water in the cup is lower than inside the egg. Water leaches out of the egg, and it collapses like a sad balloon.

The Big Eggshell Breakdown

Make egg shells disappear with a little white vinegar.

Morning milk too boring and bland? There's a fix for that.

The Rainbow Explosion!

You'll need:

Whole or 2-percent milk
Medium-size saucer
Food coloring in several hues
Cotton swabs
Rubbing alcohol
Dish soap

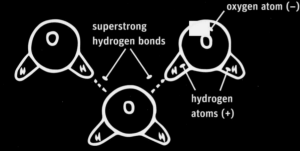

WATER MOLECULES

superstrong hydrogen bonds

oxygen atom (−)

hydrogen atoms (+)

① **Pour about ½ inch (1.25 cm)** of whole or 2-percent milk into a saucer. Let it come to room temperature.

② **Plop several drops** of different food coloring onto the milk's surface. The drops might spread a little, but they'll more or less stay where you put them.

③ **Soak the end** of a cotton swab in rubbing alcohol. Touch it to the color drops, which will quickly burst into wild whorls and mixing colors. Discard your milk rainbows after the experiment!

What's the Deal?

This swirling, whirling dance of color goes down because water molecules—and food coloring and milk, which are both mostly made of water molecules—tend to make superstrong bonds with other water molecules. (It's sorta sweet.) When it happens on the surface of a liquid, this is called *surface tension*, and the attraction between water molecules' negative and positive charges causes it. But when you add rubbing alcohol (or dish soap), its molecules break those strong bonds, making water elsewhere in the saucer pull water molecules away from the milk near the alcohol. And these water molecules bring the food coloring with them. It's the most psychedelic thing that's ever happened at breakfast!

Try This Next!

To stage a color-drop derby, set up another dish of milk, with colored drops near the center. Dip the end of a cotton swab in dish soap and then poke it into the middle of the dish. The bright blobs will race for the edges. Soap molecules bond to the water and the fat molecules in milk. How does the race differ when you use soap instead of alcohol?

1. **Fill two jars** with hot water. Load them to the brim, and then carefully keep pouring until you see the water bulge slightly on the top. Repeat with the other two containers, but this time fill them with cold water.

2. **Put a few drops** of food coloring into the bottles, choosing one color for hot water and another for cold water. Here, we used red for hot and blue for cold. Watch how the food coloring mixes. Do the colors move at different rates through the hot and cold liquids?

3. **Place an index card on** top of one of the bottles of hot water. Working over a baking pan or a sink, flip the bottle over while holding the index card in place with your hand. Then slowly take your hand away. The index card should be sealed onto the opening of the upside-down bottle.

4. **Position this bottle** so it is on top of one of the bottles of cold water with their openings lined up. The index card should be the only barrier between the two bottles.

5. **Repeat steps 3 and 4**, but this time, cover the cold bottle with an index card and flip it over to line up on top of a hot bottle.

6. **Carefully, oh so carefully,** slide the index cards out and let the waters touch. Watch the colors—do they mix or do they stay separated? Record how long it takes the colors to blend completely.

What's the Deal?

The hot (red) water and cold (blue) water stayed in separate jars in the first setup. Meanwhile, the two colors mixed to make purple in the second setup. How come? It's all about temperature's effect on *density*, the amount of *mass* (or matter) that something has in a given volume. Hot water's molecules bebop around a lot, and as a result they take up more space than their colder counterparts. So even though it looks like you filled the jars equally, there are actually fewer molecules in the hot water bottle. This means the hot water is less dense than the cold water, and when the hot water is in the bottom jar, it gets pushed to the top when the cold water sinks, creating that purple color! When the jar of cold water is on the bottom, however, the cold water stays where it is because it's denser than the hot water on top. This wet and wacky experiment demonstrates *convection*, the transfer of heat through liquid or air.

These Waters Don't Run

Suspend water with no barrier other than temperature!

You'll need:

4 identical wide-mouthed containers (baby food jars work well)

Hot water

Cold water

Food coloring in 2 hues

2 index cards

Large, shallow baking pan*

*If you don't have one, do this activity over the sink—it can get messy!

Water

This is the good stuff—the one liquid that all lifeforms need to keep going every day! Water covers 71 percent of our planet and makes up about 70 percent of our bodies. Its chemical formula is H_2O, meaning that it contains two hydrogen atoms for every one oxygen atom—and these team up to create some of the most mesmerizing, crucial stuff around . . . in the kitchen and beyond.

Billions of years ago, Earth's water may have come from outer space. When stars hatched from megaclouds of gas and dust, ice formed on the dust particles—and lucky new planet Earth probably got bombarded with lots of these tiny, icy specks. Comets and asteroids also likely helped supply us with the wet stuff, clobbering the young planet and filling newborn oceans with H_2O.

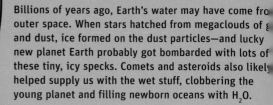

Water from space

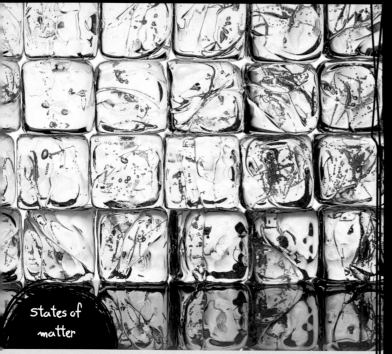

States of matter

Is it a solid? A liquid? A gas? Water can exhibit three *states of matter*. In your freezer, you'll find ice—water as a *solid*, a form in which low temperature causes the molecules to pack together in a rigid shape. Let the ice melt to experience it as you usually see it: as a *liquid*, with a loose array of molecules that hold the shape of their container and take up a fixed amount of space. Put that liquid into a pot and boil it to get *gas*: a vapor that expands to fill any space and has no fixed shape. Allow it to cool down to return it to liquid—and see the process in reverse!

Pour yourself a glass of water and float a small square paper towel on its surface. Now put a paper clip on top of the towel and watch as it sinks while the clip stays on top! This is due to water's *surface tension*: The extreme attraction between water's negatively and positively charged molecules makes a tight, hard-to-break layer on top, supporting the paper clip.

Surface tension

When you need water, you sip it from a glass. But when plants need water, they slurp it up from the ground. That's *capillary action*: Tiny tubes in the plant's stem (called *xylem*) work with water's natural surface tension to squeeze the liquid up where it's needed. To see this effect, add food coloring to a glass of water, then stick in a celery stalk or lettuce leaf. The water will carry the color up the stalk and into the leaves—and you'll get a crazy-colored snack.

Heat capacity

Capillary action

If the world gets wildly warm or shiveringly cold, species have a hard time staying alive: Their food sources disappear and their bodies struggle to adapt to extreme temperatures. But water has an incredibly high *heat capacity*, the amount of energy required to raise 1 gram of water by 1 degree Celsius. This means that water resists big changes in temperature—so fish don't boil in lakes or freeze in seas!

Universal solvent

What makes water so key in the kitchen? It is a *universal solvent*, meaning that more substances *dissolve* (break down into small particles, seeming to "disappear") in water than in any other liquid. How come? The hydrogen side of a water molecule carries a slight positive charge, while the oxygen side carries a slight negative charge. This makes other compounds want to split up and bond with water's atoms! Hence, salt, sugar, baking soda, and other ingredients can mix with water to form *solutions*—mixtures with equally distributed particles throughout.

Make Soda Erupt into Your Own Old Faithful

Prepare to step back—Mentos makes fizzy drinks explode into sky-high geysers of sugary fun foam.

You'll need:

3 2-L bottles of Diet Coke*

Selection of 2-L carbonated beverages such as Perrier, Sprite, Coke, and Dr. Pepper*

Several packs of mint Mentos*

Friend to observe and record details about the reactions

Pen and paper

*Yes, you need these specific brands for this activity! Trust us, you won't be disappointed.

① **Find a place outside** where you can make a big mess—a safe driveway or sidewalk. Ask a friend to take notes on your explosions . . . erm, experiments!

② **Place one bottle** of Diet Coke on the ground and pop off its cap. Then drop one Mentos into the bottle and back up quickly—the Diet Coke will explode into a frothy fountain, a veritable cola geyser! Have your friend measure and jot down its height and duration.

③ **Place another bottle** of Diet Coke on the ground, remove the cap, and drop in two Mentos mints. Back up quickly and, again, make a note of the stream's height and duration. Repeat once more, using three mints this time, and record what you see.

④ **Line up** the other beverages and take off their caps. Drop one Mentos into each and back up. With these bottles of fizz, do your geysers spray taller? Last longer? Have a different color or texture? Write it all down, kid scientist!

What's the Deal?

Soda is mainly a large network of water molecules with excess carbon-dioxide gas (CO_2) trapped inside. This CO_2 gets released as bubbles, but the bubbles need a place to form. Mentos have thousands of microscopic bumps on their surface, even though they feel smooth. When you drop a Mentos into Diet Coke, it provides *nucleation sites*, places where carbon-dioxide bubbles form. And the more Mentos you add, the more carbon-dioxide gas you get. Why does Diet Coke create the tallest and longest-lasting geysers? It contains aspartame and potassium benzoate, which disrupt water's high *surface tension*—the tendency for water molecules to bond together and resist anything that tries to break them apart. Molecules in the Mentos can also reduce this surface tension and really let the bubbles fly!

Mentos's many nucleation sites

CO_2 gas forms on the Mentos and bubbles up

41

What's the Deal?

When you put certain substances into water, they can lose a hydrogen ion (which converts them to an *acid*) or gain a hydrogen ion (typical of a *base*). To discover whether a substance is an acid or a base (also called *alkaline*), we test its pH level using an *indicator*: a chemical that changes color when it comes into contact with an acid or a base. What makes cabbage juice such a good indicator, if not a good beverage? Its cells contain a water-soluble purple pigment called *anthocyanin*, which turns red in an acidic environment and bluish-green in an alkaline environment. Acids have a low pH, anywhere from 1 to 6, and they show up as reds, pinks, or purples when they mix with an indicator. Lemon juice, vinegar, and soda are all acids. Bases, on the other hand, have a high pH, ranging from 8 to 14. They appear blue, green, or yellow with an indicator. Common examples include baking soda, soapy water, and bleach. (Water is neutral, if you were wondering, with a pH level that falls smack dab in the middle at 7!)

1 **Fill the blender** nearly to the top with cabbage. Add water to the halfway mark and blend on high until it's a cabbage smoothie. (Don't drink it—it has a higher calling!)

2 **Pour the smoothie** through the strainer to remove large bits and store it in a 2-L bottle. This is your *indicator*—the chemical compound you will add to a solution to visually determine its pH.

3 **Place your glasses** in a row and fill each one halfway with the indicator.

4 **Choose one** of your test chemicals (say, vinegar or baking soda) and guess whether it's an acid, with a low pH, or a base, with a high pH. Then pour a little of it into one of the glasses. If the solution turns red, your test chemical is an acid. If it turns green, it's a base.

5 **Try each test chemical,** arranging the glasses from reddest to greenest. Then try taking your most acidic solution and slowly adding a base. The solution will turn back into the indicator's original purple color. That's because you've *neutralized* it, returning the solution's pH to 7.

Try This Next!

Take your experiment on the road by making your own pH test strips. Soak coffee filters in the indicator and let them dry, and then cut them into strips. You can use these strips to find out the pH of any liquid—simply dip one into the liquid and watch the paper change color. Try testing your friends' drinks at lunch, or experimenting with different antacid brands to see which really neutralizes acids the best.

The Red-Cabbage Reveal

Make your own pH indicator—a scientist's tool that tells an acid from a base.

Vinegar **2**

Lemon juice **4**

Water **7**

Baking soda or Alka-Seltzer **9**

Ammonia **11**

Laundry detergent **13**

You'll need:

Blender

Head of purple cabbage, cut into chunks

Water

Strainer

2-L bottle

Several clear drinking glasses or test tubes

Test chemicals*

Large white coffee filters

*Vinegar, lemon juice, water, ammonia (make sure you check with an adult before grabbing this stuff!), laundry detergent, and baking soda or Alka-Seltzer are all great starters!

Explore Natural Dyes

Stain fabric with your food . . . on purpose this time!

You'll need:

Alum*

Cream of tartar

Water

Pot or saucepan

Undyed and unbleached natural fabric, such as cotton or wool

Apron

Onion skins, carrot tops, beets, blueberries, hibiscus tea, black tea, and/or coffee grounds

Rubber gloves

Herbs

Paper towels

Masking tape

Hammer

Iron

½ cup (150 g) salt

*You can often find alum in the spice section of your grocery store, or buy it online.

1. **Prepare your mordant,** a metallic salt solution that will help your natural dye fix to whatever fabric you choose. (Think of it as glue for colors!) Put 0.07 ounces (2 g) of alum, 0.035 ounces (1 g) of cream of tartar, and ½ cup (120 mL) of water in a pot or saucepan. Choose at least two fabrics, dampen them with water, and then submerge them in the pot. Let them simmer for 30 minutes.

2. **Don your apron,** and then pick a few sources of natural dye and chop them up. Let each source steep in its own hot-water bath for 15 to 30 minutes. (You may want to simmer them over heat.) The longer you leave the dye sources, the deeper your color will be.

3. **When the fabric pieces** have finished mordanting, put on rubber gloves and remove the fabric from the pot. Pat the fabric pieces with paper towels to eliminate any drips, and then divide them up among your dye baths. Let them sit for at least 15 minutes. Again, the longer you leave them, the more vivid the color will be. Once you're satisfied, give the fabric a good rinse. How well has the fabric absorbed each dye?

Try This Next!

You can also pound out natural herb dyes with a hammer. Lay out paper towels, and then place an undyed fabric piece already soaked in a mordant on top. Secure the herbs to the fabric with masking tape. Flip the piece over so the herbs are sandwiched between the paper towel and the fabric. Hammer until you see the green color come through the cloth. Iron and soak it in a mix of ½ cup (150 g) salt and 8 cups (2 L) cold water to set the pattern.

What's the Deal?

Before people figured out how to make chemical dyes in the laboratory, plants and animals were our only sources for coloring fabric—and they're still great sources today. They contain chemical groups that can bind to a *substrate*, such as a natural fabric, yarn, or leather. The chemicals form ionic or hydrogen bonds with a charged portion of the fabric, such as the keratin found in wool or the cellulose found in cotton. Mordants act as bridges that form stronger covalent bonds between the dye molecules and the fabric. These molecules allow multiple dye molecules to bond to one substrate site, allowing for a deeper, longer-lasting color.

See Your Food Glow

Turns out boring old spinach has a vivid secret inside.

1. **Bring a pot** of water to a boil, and then add the greens and let them boil for 1 minute. Remove the greens with tongs and plunge them into the ice bath.

2. **Place the cooled greens** into the blender and add 2 tablespoons of vegetable oil. Blend until you have a thin green liquid. (Add more oil to keep it fluid, if needed.)

3. **Strain the liquid** through the sieve into a glass. Give it a good look—you should have a bright green liquid.

4. **Turn out the lights** and switch on the black light, and then hold it above the oil. The oil will suddenly glow blood red!

5. **To see this experiment** in a different way, grab a jar of olive oil (which contains concentrated chlorophyll), kill the lights, and point a green laser into the jar. What color is the green beam as it passes through the olive oil?

What's the Deal?

Chlorophyll is the general name for a class of green pigment molecules in plants. These molecules have the property of *fluorescence*, which means they absorb light from one point of the spectrum and re-emit it in another. The different chlorophylls that you see here absorb light from the ultraviolet and blue range and re-emit it as bright red.

Try This Next!

Time to turn your black light on the contents of your fridge and pantry. Wave it over tonic water, milk, and perfectly ripe bananas to see a range of luminous blues and purples. What other fluorescent foods can you find? For a glowing treat, replace the water in Jell-O with tonic water, and ta-da—you've got a brilliant dessert!

You'll need:

Pot

Water

Big handful of greens (such as spinach,
kale, mint, parsley, or cilantro)

Tongs

Ice bath (bowl filled with ice and water)

Vegetable oil

Blender

Fine-mesh sieve

Black light

Olive oil

Green laser

Box of Jell-O

Tonic water

Return of the Veggies

They keep on growing—there's no stopping them!

You'll need:

A sunny spot

Several clear, flat-bottomed glass or plastic containers

Veggies such as green and red onions, sweet potatoes, lettuce, and garlic—plus others you find and want to try!

Wooden skewers or toothpicks

Turns out vegetables don't just grow from seeds—they can also regenerate from leftover scraps. Called *vegetative reproduction,* this process involves soaking the roots, stems, leaves, or bulbs in water for a few days, and then transferring them to the soil in your backyard or into a pot to grow into real veggies. What other plants can you bring back from scraps? Try pineapples, carrots, ginger, and more in your windowsill garden!

1 **Start by scouting** a spot by a bright windowsill in your kitchen—this is where you'll position your food-scrap garden and watch it sprout new delectations.

2 **Next, gather an assortment** of glasses, small bowls, and flat-bottomed containers for your veggie scraps. Clear containers are ideal—you want sunlight to reach the veggie inside the container.

3 **Save veggie scraps!** Look for *tubers* (fleshy foods that grow underground, such as sweet potatoes) and plants with *bulbs* (round bits with papery white scales, such as green onions and garlic). You can also experiment with foods that sprout from clippings of their stems (such as lettuce, celery, and leeks).

4 **Start with bulbs** from green onions and garlic. Submerge them in individual glasses of water, place them in your sunny spot, and change the water daily. In a few days, you'll see green tips bursting through!

5 **Next, try some tubers.** Organic sweet potatoes will generate new roots and leaves from growths called *slips*. To give one of these sweet spuds a jumpstart, stick wooden skewers or toothpicks into it, and then prop it on a glass's edge so it's suspended in water. After a few weeks, you'll see roots—a sign that your sweet potato is ready for planting!

6 **For plants that grow from stems** (such as lettuce), place the base in a flat-bottomed container in the sun. Check daily, spraying with water and changing out the liquid in the container occasionally. Soon you'll see little leaves growing from the stem. The same trick works with the base of an onion, which you can transfer into soil to completely regrow.

49

1. **Scavenge food scraps** for your terrarium after dinner. Look for lots of food types, but skip meat. Cut up big pieces so they fit in your container.

2. **Dip each piece of food** into water and put it into your container. Spread the pieces out so that they are close to each other but not in a heap—you want sneak peeks at your mildewing masterpiece as it develops!

3. **Put the lid** on and tape around the edge to seal it. On a label, write "Mold terrarium—do not touch! (That means you)" and stick it to your container. Put it in a safe place.

4. **Every day,** look at your mold terrarium, jotting down notes about what you see. Some foods might grow a blue-green powder; others might create a gray-white fuzz. After a while, you may see black dots, or molds spreading from one food to another!

What's the Deal?

That fuzzy fur you see is a type of *fungus*, a large group of organisms, many of which eat decaying things. Mold grows from tiny floating spores that luck out and land on damp food, where they feast and grow into the strangely eye-pleasing stuff in your garbage! Mold also makes chemicals that help break down the food even more. There are even some molds that we eat—like the types in certain cheeses.

1. Spores float near the food and land on it.

2. Spores grow into large filaments (*hyphae*), and then they clump together to form a *mycelium*, which absorbs nutrients.

3. Mycelia release more mold spores into the air, and the cycle begins again!

5. **After two weeks,** throw the entire terrarium away. (Don't open it! It's not good to smell, eat, or breathe in mold.)

Try This Next!

Choose any packaged cookie, cake, or granola bar. Following the same steps, prepare and place it into a fresh mold terrarium. Observe the rate and type of mold growth. How does it vary from fresh food? Many packaged foods have added preservatives to keep food from breaking down easily. How might that affect your results?

Your Leftovers Make a Fungus Feast

Assemble a mold terrarium and watch fungus eat the food you didn't.

You'll need:

Leftover food, such as bread, fruit, vegetables, cheese, cookies, or cake

Knife

Water

Big glass jar or clear plastic container with lid*

Duct tape

Label

Permanent marker

*Make sure it's okay to throw away the container after your experiment!

Spices

Long ago, the contents of your kitchen's spice rack changed not just cooking but the world. Once people discovered the big flavors, preservative powers, and medicinal values packed inside nuts, seeds, bark, and roots, food got better—and global trade routes opened so these tasty treasures could be shared. Each spice has a unique taste . . . and is a unique scientific morsel, too!

These delicate orange threads are the stigma of the crocus flower. Each flower has only three stigma, which workers must harvest by hand—making saffron one of the most expensive spices around. It gets its vivid color from *carotenoids* (the same molecules that make carrots orange). You only need to soak a few of these strands to release saffron's color, flavor, and aroma.

Saffron

Spearmint and caraway

Who knew tree bark could be so delicious? Harvested from the inside bark of trees in the *Cinnamomum* genus and allowed to dry and curl into "quills," cinnamon gets its strong, sweet spiciness from the chemical compound *cinnamaldehyde*. The priciest stuff (Ceylon cinnamon) comes from Sri Lanka.

Next time you're in the produce aisle, take a good whiff of spearmint (large photo above), and then dart to the spices section and sniff caraway seeds (small inset photo). They smell nothing alike, but they both get their distinct flavors from the same molecule: *carvone*. One crucial difference in each spice's carvone makes them taste different: The molecular structure is the same but it is flipped left to right, so carvone's structure in caraway mirrors the structure of the carvone in spearmint, and vice versa. Scientists call this *chirality*.

Cinnamon

Ever wonder why chili powder, hot sauce, and jalapeño peppers seem to set your mouth ablaze? They contain *capsaicin*, a compound that triggers the sensory neurons typically activated by extreme heat—which makes your brain think that your tongue is on fire. Spiciness is rated using the Scoville scale, a special system that measures how much you can dilute a food's capsaicin before humans cease to register it as tongue-scorching hot.

Pepper

Chili powder

The world's most traded spice, black pepper starts out as a berry that, once dried, is called a *peppercorn*. It's then ground into the fine granules that you sprinkle on your food. Ever sneezed after dusting a dish with it? That's because pepper contains the chemical *piperine*, an irritant that bothers the mucous membrane in your nose and makes you go "Achoo!"

Ginger

While it may look like a root, this funky, knobby little foodstuff is actually a *rhizome*, or an underground stem. You can scarf it down fresh or use it as a dried powder, and you'll find it in everything from curries to candies, and pickles to soda. It gets its curious, zesty tang from the compound *gingerol*—which many believe to have medicinal benefits.

Get in a Pickle

Turns out there's more than one way
to make snappy, tangy pickled treats.

1. **First up,** let's make pickles using *fermentation*, a process in which micro-organisms eat natural sugars and make lactic acid, preserving cucumbers and giving them that tangy taste! Scrub the pickling cucumbers in cool water, and then trim their blossom ends. (You can also pickle carrots, beets, and other veggies once you get a batch under your belt.)

2. **Put half the pickling spices** and 1 bunch of dill in the plastic bucket or crock. Add in the cukes.

3. **To make your brine,** mix the white vinegar, pickling salt, and water so that the salt dissolves completely. Then pour the vinegar mixture over the cucumbers. Add in the garlic and the remaining spices and dill.

4. **Avoiding spoilage is crucial,** so fully submerge your cukes in the brine by placing a glass or ceramic plate (no metal!) on top of them to keep them from floating. Cover the crock tightly with its lid during fermentation so bad microbes don't spoil the batch. The ideal temperature is between 70°F and 75°F (21–24°C).

5. **Check your cucumbers** every day. Skim off any film growing on top and keep the pickles completely covered with brine, adding more brine if needed.

6. **Let the cucumbers ferment** for 2½ to 3 weeks until they're olive green or evenly translucent. Don't exceed a total time of 3 weeks. When finished, store your pickles in any container in your fridge.

Turn the page ⟶

You'll need:

5 pounds (2.25 kg) pickling cucumbers
⅛ cup (20 g) whole mixed pickling spices
2 bunches fresh dill
3-gallon (11.5-L) plastic bucket or crock with lid
½ cup (120 mL) white vinegar
¼ cup plus 2 tablespoons (110 g) coarse pickling salt
½ gallon (2 L) water
5 fresh garlic cloves, peeled
Glass or ceramic plate
1 fresh cucumber
Large plastic syringe
Apple cider or seasoned rice vinegar

7 Next up, experiment with a technique called *flash pickling*, in which you submerge cukes in a liquid-filled chamber (in this case, a syringe filled with rice vinegar), reduce the pressure in the chamber, and then repressurize the container to "pickle" the cukes. Start by chopping the cucumber into small pieces and place several inside the syringe tube.

8 Insert and depress the plunger to squeeze out as much air as possible, and then draw up vinegar from a bowl so the liquid covers all the pieces.

9 Point the syringe up and push out all the air, and then tap or flick it a few times to get rid of any remaining air.

10 Hold your thumb over the syringe's tip to seal it, and use the other hand to pull back hard on the plunger. Release and push out any air that appeared, and then pull back and release the plunger again. This causes the vinegar to rush into the cucumber pieces!

11 Remove the plunger and empty the syringe. Sample your quick pickles! Do they taste like the ones that took 3 weeks? Enjoy them lickety-split or store them in your fridge.

What's the Deal?

Fermentation is the crucial process behind a lot of our favorite foods, including bread, yogurt, and cheese. In this case, it allows good microorganisms to thrive, giving pickles their sour tang and making pickled food last months longer than the un-pickled versions! Also important is *osmosis*, a process in which substances move through a membrane from an area of high concentration to one of low concentration. Think of it this way: That cucumber has a lot of water inside, but the salty brine it swims in contains less water. So the water inside the cuke travels through its skin into the brine, creating a crunchy pickle. But what about the flash-pickled batch? You have Boyle's law to thank for that quick treat. When you pull on the plunger, you reduce the pressure inside the syringe, and the air inside increases in volume. The air inside the pickle cells bursts them open, and when you release the plunger, the brine floods into the space where the air used to be!

OSMOSIS IN PICKLING

1. A high concentration of water molecules (H_2O) are trapped in the pickle's cells.

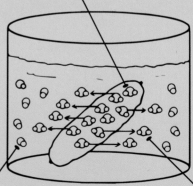

NaCl

2. Water molecules flow into the surrounding salty brine, where there's a lower concentration of H_2O molecules.

H_2O

Dance Up a Batch of Butter

A little shake-rattle-roll is all you need for smooth, buttery goodness. Who knew?

You'll need:

Several marbles

Several glass or plastic jars (baby food jars are great)

1 cup (235 mL) heavy cream

Parsley, chives, garlic, or orange zest

1. **Put one marble** in each jar. Divide the heavy cream among the jars and seal each one tightly—you don't want to fling dairy products all over the kitchen.

2. **Time to shake it!** We mean it—shake the jars like crazy. The marbles will fly around inside, as will the cream. You can share the shaking with a friend, or carefully roll them on the ground.

3. **At first you'll hear** the marble kicking around inside the jar. When you've been shaking it for a while, it'll start to get quiet and then hush up completely. Keep shaking and soon you'll see a chunk of butter starting to form.

4. **Once you've got a good clump,** remove the marble, give your butter a rinse, and spread it on a slice of bread near you!

What's the Deal?

Heavy cream is an *emulsion*: a substance that occurs when droplets of one type of liquid float in another without mixing together. The fat molecules in heavy cream don't mix with the water molecules; they prefer to stay suspended as distinct globules without bonding to any H_2O! But when you shake the heavy cream, those fat molecules slam together and—if they slam hard enough—they start to stick together and form butter. The marble helps speed up that process and gives the fat something to gather around. The fat glob gets bigger and bigger until there is a ball of mostly fat with some water molecules mixed in, and you have a delicious spread.

Try This Next!

Your fresh butter tastes great, but you can customize it! Chop up some herbs (parsley or chives work well, but garlic or orange zest are tasty, too). Roll a very cold butter cylinder into the herbs, pressing down firmly to get the leaves to stick.

1 Heat 1 quart (1 L) of milk in a pot over medium heat until it reaches 180°F (82°C)—or until the milk starts to froth. Stir the milk continuously so it doesn't scald your pot.

2 Take the milk off the heat, letting it cool to between 110°F and 115°F (43–46°C). (To speed up this process, try placing the pot in a sink filled with ice water.)

3 Remove your starter (aka the store-bought yogurt) from the fridge and let it warm to room temperature. Thoroughly stir 4 tablespoons of the store-bought yogurt into your milk.

4 Make a hot-water bath in a cooler that will insulate the milk-yogurt mixture and keep it between 110°F and 115°F (43–46°C).

5 Portion the mix into small cups, and place them in the bath for 8 to 12 hours. If you prefer thicker yogurt, strain the mixture through a cheesecloth, or stash it in the fridge overnight.

You'll need:

1 quart (1 L) milk
Pot or saucepan
Thermometer
Wooden spoon or whisk
4 tablespoons plain, unsweetened yogurt
Insulated cooler
Cups

What's the Deal?

Yogurt is actually alive—it's teeming with bacteria that love to eat *lactose*, a protein found in milk. When they gobble up this protein, they create lactic acid. This chemical gives yogurt its thick, creamy texture and tangy flavor. When you put the yogurt into a hot-water bath, you provide this bacteria with an incubator. Since these good bacteria love heat, the hot bath helps nurture them and allows them to thrive and grow.

Whip Up Yogurt

Go ahead—invite some bacteria over for breakfast.

What's the Deal?

Dry ice looks like movie magic, but it's really just carbon dioxide (CO_2) in solid form. Unlike typical ice, dry ice doesn't melt as it warms; instead, it *sublimates*, skipping from a solid form directly into a gas. That gas is very, very cold, and it causes a drop in temperature in the surrounding air—condensing water vapor into the chilly fog you see! When dry ice meets your ice-cream mixture, it freezes the mix so fast that large ice crystals don't have a chance to form, making your treat supersmooth. By the time you eat the ice cream, the carbon dioxide has floated away, and all that remains is the sweet taste of science.

1 **Ready your recipe!** (We've included a chocolate ice cream recipe here, but you can make any flavor you like with this technique!) Start by whisking together the cocoa powder and sugars, and then add the milk and mix until the sugar dissolves. Gently stir in the heavy cream and vanilla extract.

2 **Cover the bowl** with plastic wrap and stick it in the fridge for at least 2 hours or overnight. You want it to be nice and cold.

3 **Time for dry ice!** Some strong words of caution here, kid scientist: Your grown-up must help you with this step, and everyone must wear safety goggles and gloves and use tongs! Wrap the dry ice in a towel and strike it with a mallet to break it into small pieces. Then put the pieces into a food processor or blender and reduce them to a fine powder; it'll look like snow when it's good to go.

4 **Pour the cold cream mix** into a stand mixer with a paddle attachment. Slowly start adding the powdered dry ice—there will be tons of vapor!

5 **Mix on** a low speed until the ice cream is frozen. If it starts to look liquidy, stop the mixer and add more dry ice powder.

6 **Practice patience.** Put the ice cream in the fridge for one day so the dry ice can dissipate. Then give your tongue a real treat—a supersmooth frosty chocolate sensation!

You'll need:

¾ cup (85 g) unsweetened cocoa powder
½ cup (100 g) sugar
⅓ cup (65 g) packed dark brown sugar
1 cup (235 mL) whole milk
2 cups (470 mL) heavy cream
½ tablespoon vanilla extract
Bowl
Plastic wrap
Safety goggles and gloves
Tongs
60 ounces (1,500 g) dry ice*
Towel
Mallet
Food processor or blender
Stand mixer with paddle attachment

*Available at most supermarkets.

Spooky Fast Ice Cream

Here's the most chilling ice-cream technique under the sun.

Dairy

Did you know that butter, cheese, sour cream, yogurt, and ice cream all come from milk—the protein-rich liquid created in the mammary glands of all mammals? This essential elixir provides the young of many species with the nutrients they need for a strong start. It also contains powerful microbacteria that move right in and establish a healthy gut. Milk is so important that humans have come up with a wealth of ways to enjoy it. Check out a few here!

When superspicy food sets your mouth on fire, get milk! The capsaicin in chiles makes your tongue feel like it's burning. Dairy contains *casein*, a protein that will bind with capsaicin to relieve the sting. Try a *lassi* (a yogurt drink from India) with your next five-alarm curry.

Cooling casein

Moldy cheese

Generally, we drink either cow, sheep, or goat's milk. But humans also consume milk from camels, reindeer, water buffalo, horses, and yaks. (To milk a reindeer, you need two people—one to hold its horns, the other to milk!) The taste and amount of milk that each creature yields varies, with cows leading the pack at an impressive 6½ gallons (25 L) a day.

When it comes to cheeses that get their flavor from fungi, the kid jury is still out as to whether they deserve an "Ew!" or a "Yum!" To create blue cheese, cheesemakers introduce penicillium. The mold grows as the cheese cures, causing the trademark blue veins, tangy flavor, and stinky smell. To make the blue veins run throughout, they poke the cheese with needles to let air inside to feed the mold. The more air holes, the more mold grows—and the bluer (and stinkier) your cheese!

Milk sources

Curds and whey

Keeping milk fresh used to be a big problem: Bacteria love milk, and given the chance, they move in, spoil it, and make people sick. In 1846, Louis Pasteur discovered that if you heat a liquid to just below boiling, you'll kill these microbes. Today, much raw milk gets heated at a high temperature for a short amount of time, extending its safety and shelf life. Thanks, Louis!

Pasteurization

So how do you get from a glass of cool milk to a round of cheese so hard you slice through it? First, cheesemakers introduce a starter bacteria to feast on the lactose in the milk, creating the lactic acid that will give the cheese its taste. Then they add an acid, such as lemon juice, or an enzyme-rich substance called *rennet* to separate the milk into *curds* (solid bits of the protein casein) and *whey* (the leftover runny liquid). The curds are then strained, cured, and allowed to "ripen" so their flavors emerge.

Lactose intolerance

Sadly, we can't all enjoy milk's many delights—some people get a tummy ache from ice cream! That's because they are *lactose intolerant*: Their bodies cannot digest a sugar in dairy called *lactose*. Usually, an *enzyme* (a protein that helps in chemical reactions) breaks lactose into the simple sugars glucose and galactose, which our bodies easily digest. Lactose-intolerant people don't have enough of this enzyme (called lactase), so dairy makes them ill. They often opt for dairy alternatives, such as almond or soy milk.

Oozerific Ooze-a-thon

This confused goop doesn't know if it's a liquid or a solid—which makes it extra fun to squeeze, pour, run across, and dance with!

1 **Cover your counter** or table with newspaper—this one is going to get messy. Dump 1 cup (125 g) cornstarch into your bowl. Then slowly pour in ½ cup (120 mL) of water and a few drops of food coloring. Mix the cornstarch and water with your fingers until it's completely combined. Pour this goop (called *oobleck*) out onto the tray.

2 **Try tapping the surface** with your finger or a spoon. If you've got the ratio just right (about 2 parts cornstarch to 1 part water), the mixture won't splash. Instead, it'll feel surprisingly rubbery and solid. Add more cornstarch if the oobleck mixture is too wet, more water if it's too powdery.

3 **You've made your ooze**—time to play! Pick up a handful and give it a good squeeze. Now stop squeezing. Watch as the mixture drips through your fingers!

4 **Now rest your fingers** on the ooze's surface. Let them sink down to the bottom of the tray. Then try to pull them out fast. What happens? Does the ooze quickly harden on your hands?

5 **Next, take a blob** and roll it between your hands to make a ball. Then stop rolling it. The ooze will trickle between your fingers.

6 **Bring some objects** into the mix! Put a small plastic toy on the surface. Does it stay there or does it sink? Try pushing a

fork through the gunk. Does the ooze part and let it pass, or does it freeze up so the fork struggles to get through? Now scoop up some oobleck and watch it solidify as strings of it swing through the air.

7 **Now make it huge.** Go outside and set up a small plastic or inflatable pool, and then prepare a new mixture of cornstarch and water at roughly a 2:1 ratio. How much you need depends on the size of the pool, but you'll want to create ooze at least 3 inches (7.5 cm) deep.

8 **Once you've made your mixture,** it's time to walk on it! If you jump into the pool and run, the ooze will act as a solid and you won't sink. If you jump in the pool and then stand still, the ooze will initially

Turn the page ⟹

You'll need:

Newspaper
1 cup (125 g) cornstarch
Large bowl
½ cup (120 mL) water
Food coloring
Tray
Fork or spoon
Small toy
Small plastic or inflatable pool
Stereo speaker
Plastic wrap

act as a solid but then it will liquefy, allowing you to sink. How many steps can you take on the ooze? How long can you stay on top of it?

9 **To dispose of this good gooeyness,** try putting some in zipper-lock bags and handing it out to buddies, as it keeps pretty much indefinitely in the fridge. If you must throw it out, let it dry and then chuck it in the garbage.

What's the Deal?

Your ooze is made up of tiny, solid particles of cornstarch suspended in water. Chemists call this type of mixture a *colloid*, and this one behaves strangely indeed! When you bang on your ooze with a spoon or quickly squeeze a handful, it acts like a solid. The harder you push, the thicker it becomes. But when you open your hand, the ooze drips like a liquid. Try to stir the ooze quickly with a finger and it'll resist your movement. But stir it slowly and it'll flow around your finger easily. The ooze acts this way because of its *viscosity*, or resistance to flow. You'll note that water's viscosity doesn't change when you stir, but the viscosity of your ooze does. In the eighteenth century, Isaac Newton identified the properties of an ideal liquid. Water and other liquids that have these properties are called *Newtonian fluids*. Your ooze doesn't, so it's what's called a *non-Newtonian fluid*. There are many types of non-Newtonian fluids— ketchup is another one!

Try This Next!

Get your ooze to dance! First, ask your grown-up for permission to let you anywhere near the stereo equipment with your goop in hand. (We're serious—you're on your own if you attempt this activity without parental okay first!) Whip up another batch of oobleck, this time making it a bit thicker: 2 cups (250 g) of cornstarch to 1 cup (235 mL) of water should do the trick. Next, have your grown-up remove the subwoofer (the conical part of the speaker) from the housing. Then secure a piece of plastic wrap over the subwoofer to keep it clean, though this stuff wipes up nicely with a wet rag. Find a subwoofer test tone online and try it out on your speaker. Finally, with the speaker turned off, carefully pour the new batch of ooze onto the plastic wrap. Now you're ready to turn the speaker back on, play the test tone again, and watch the ooze dance around like crazy! Vary frequencies and volume and see the differences in the oobleck's dancing. (We find that a frequency of around 25 hertz works best.)

Mini-fy with a Pressure Cooker

No shrink-ray gun required.

You'll need:

Pressure cooker
Water
Small heatproof bowl
Styrofoam cup*
Timer
Pot holder
Tongs

*Styrofoam takes a long time to biodegrade.
See if you can find old Styrofoam cups
instead of buying new ones.

1 **Ask your grown-up** to help you use the pressure cooker, a neat kitchen appliance that looks like a pot with a lock on it. This device lets you seal in food, liquid, and air while the pot is over heat, making the food cook at a much faster rate than it normally would.

2 **Cover the bottom** of the pressure cooker with 1 inch (2.5 cm) of water and place it on a stove burner.

3 **Position a small heatproof bowl** inside the pot. Take your Styrofoam cup and place it inside the bowl so it stands upright.

4 **Now it's time** to put on the pressure! Put the lid on the pressure cooker and lock it. Turn on the burner at full force and wait for the telltale screech or hiss of the pressure cooker. Once you've heard it, set a timer for 15 minutes. (You may need to experiment a little to see how long your specific pressure cooker takes to shrink the cup!)

5 **This next step** is for your grown-up, as pressure cookers are pretty serious business and can be dangerous. When the time is up, your grown-up should turn off the burner and hit the release valve on the pressure cooker. That will start to release the pressure inside the pot—you'll hear the sound of it escaping.

6 **Allow the pressure cooker** to cool. (It's a good idea for your grown-up to run cool water over it in the sink.) Then have your grown-up remove the lid using a pot holder.

7 **Grab a pair of tongs** and reach inside the pressure cooker—you should come up with a teeny-tiny Styrofoam cup! How much smaller is it than the usual cup? See any other changes in texture or shape?

1. The air inside Styrofoam's tightly packed, inflated plastic beads . . .

2. . . . gets squeezed out in the pressure cooker, making the cup shrink!

What's the Deal?

Pressure cookers create a high-pressure environment that allows food to cook at higher temperatures than normal, which means they also cook more quickly. But why would that make the cup shrink, you ask? Styrofoam is made of tiny synthetic plastic beads that have been inflated with air. When you heat up the cup in the pressure cooker, the air inside the beads get squeezed, which shrinks the cup!

DIY Density Column

Stack up liquids of different densities to see which comes out on top.

You'll need:

3 small containers
Water
70 percent isopropyl alcohol
91 percent isopropyl alcohol
Food coloring in three hues
Graduated cylinder
Eyedropper
Canola oil
Mineral oil

1. **Pour at least 50 mL** each of the water, 60 percent isopropyl alcohol, and 91 percent isopropyl alcohol into the three separate containers. (For the 60 percent, buy 70 percent isopropyl alcohol and dilute it by adding 2 mL of water for every 10 mL of the alcohol.)

2. **Tint each liquid** with 1 drop of food coloring so you can tell them apart. Label the containers if it helps you remember their contents.

3. **Time to stack!** Using an eyedropper, slowly and carefully transfer the colored water from its container to the graduated cylinder. Make sure that you don't get any of the liquid on the cylinder's walls. (Rinse the eyedropper between every transfer of each liquid).

4. **Next, drizzle the canola oil** into the cylinder. It helps to use the tick marks on your graduated cylinder as a guide so you pour equal portions of water and oil. Watch to see if the two liquids mix.

5. **Add the 60 percent isopropyl alcohol.** Spot any mingling of the different-colored fluids?

6. **Pour in the mineral oil** and monitor for any transfer of liquid within the density column.

7. **Top it off** with 91 percent isopropyl alcohol. Be careful when handling this substance, as it's typically used as a disinfectant and can irritate your skin.

What's the Deal?

The liquids don't mix at all—they stay stacked in layers! That's because the liquids have very different *densities* (the amount of mass a substance has divided by its volume) and you've poured them in order of most to least dense. With water—our heavyweight—at the bottom, the slightly less dense canola oil floats on top. (It helps that water won't mix with oil, since water molecules are *polar*—they have a slight electrical charge—and oil molecules are *nonpolar*, so they have no charge.) The 60 percent isopropyl alcohol solution floats on the oil, and so on, until we reach the ultra-light 91 percent isopropyl alcohol.

Try This Next!

Add an element of mystery! Invite some friends over to experiment with the different liquids—but don't tell them which order will result in a perfectly stacked tower, or which liquids will mix with the food coloring. (Hint: Since the food coloring is water-based, the oils won't mingle with it.) Once they've figured out the winning order, try dropping objects of various weights into the column. How far down will a nail sink? Or a marble?

Not all cooking requires heat! You can prepare fish and infuse it with flavor—all with the cooking power of simple citrus.

Stupendous Ceviche

1 **Combine the lime juice**, coconut milk, and salt in the bowl. Add the jalapeño, yellow bell pepper, cucumber, tomato, green onions, cilantro, and lime zest. Then add the chopped tuna. Stir well to coat all the ingredients in the juice.

2 **Cover the bowl** with plastic wrap and put it in the fridge. When you first put it in, the fish is slippery and raw. After just 1 minute, the fish will be flavored but still uncooked. After 2 minutes, the fish will show some changes in exterior texture. Five minutes in, and you can prod it with a fork to discover that it's firmer, but not perfect yet. After 10 minutes, it starts to hit the sweet spot: firm on the outside, but tender inside. From here on, it's up to your personal taste when it's ideal to eat.

3 **When the fish** has the desired texture, take the bowl out and serve the ceviche on butter lettuce leaves. But leave at least one spoonful in a bowl in the fridge and check on it over the next 2 hours. After

What's the Deal?

Notice how the fish's texture changes during its time in the fridge? It went in raw but came out "cooked"! The changes in color and texture are called *protein denaturation*. That's when the long strands of protein stretch out and form an extensive protein network. That protein network affects the final texture of the food and is responsible for meats getting tougher the longer you cook them. In ceviche it's not heat but acidic lime juice that does the cooking. It's a form of pickling that denatures the fish's protein. The process of marination doesn't kill all pathogens, so it's important to use fresh fish and eat the dish right away.

30 minutes, the fish will be nearly too cooked—it'll be all dried out. At the 2-hour mark, the fish will be so overcooked that it will fall apart! Discard this fish when your investigations are complete.

| Raw | 1 minute | 2 minutes | 5 minutes | 10 minutes | 30 minutes | 1 hour |

The Great Dinner Dissection

Snag a chicken leg before it's cooked and explore how tendons work.

You'll need:

Gloves (latex or plastic)

Raw chicken drumstick and thigh (skin on) that are still attached to each other

Chopping board

Sharp knife (a craft knife or scalpel will also do!)

1. **Put on your gloves** and place the chicken leg on a chopping board. Always be careful with raw poultry: Keep the chicken confined to the chopping board and always wash your hands, cutting board, and knife afterward! Chicken—though safe to eat when cooked—contains nasty critters that can make humans sick if ingested raw.

2. **First up,** look at the skin, noting its texture, color, and the bumps where the bird's feathers used to be. Tug the skin loose and roll it off the leg. Check out the exposed fat and thin connective tissue between the skin and flesh, and look for *capillaries*: tiny vessels that supply blood to organs and tissues. Tug on the tendons to see how the bones move. The chicken's muscles would normally do this tugging.

3. **With a Knife,** slice the drumstick from where it meets the thigh to the base. Cut through the muscles and *tendons* (cords of tissue that join muscles to bones) at the base and untwist the muscle groups—which are entwined kind of like a rope! Count the muscle layers and look for blood vessels.

4. **Slice at the Joint** where the drumstick and thigh connect. Find the tough bands of tissue, called *ligaments*, that hold the joint together. Look for the *fat pads* (cushions of flesh that help absorb impact) and *cartilage caps* (protective coverings) on the bones. Examine how the bones fit together and what connects them.

What's the Deal?

Your leg has a lot in common with the chicken leg you just dissected! Tendons, the tough strands you saw at the "knee" of your chicken leg, are strong bands of tissue that bind muscles to bones and control your movements. For example, muscles in your palm and wrist, bound together by tendons, control your finger bones. Look at the back of your hand and wiggle your index finger. See the slim line moving over your knuckle? That's a tendon in action. Tendons are so strong that your bones will usually break before your tendons tear! Ligaments help further by holding it all together—they connect the finger bones to the hand bones, the hand bones to the wrist bones, the wrist bones to the arm bones, and so on.

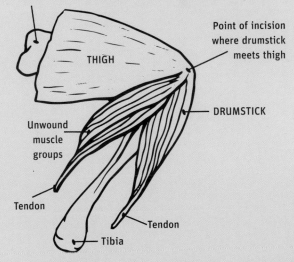

Femur

THIGH

Point of incision where drumstick meets thigh

DRUMSTICK

Unwound muscle groups

Tendon

Tendon

Tibia

The Wonderful World of Seeds

Every plant we eat comes from these tiny packets of genetic info. Collect some and see what's inside!

You'll need:

Paper towel

Tray or cookie sheet

Different types of fruits and veggies, such as strawberries, bell peppers, tomatoes, watermelons, peaches, squashes—anything's game!

Snack seeds, such as sunflower seeds (in their husks), pumpkin seeds, and poppy seeds

A few large beans, such as kidney or pinto

Handheld magnifying glass

Small paring knife

What's the Deal?

A seed is a little life-support package with three main parts: a *seed coat* (the tough covering), the *cotyledon* (food supply), and an *embryonic plant*. You may not be able to see it in every seed, but the embryonic plant contains the *plumule* (the baby leaves), *epicotyl* (which will soon be the shoot), *hypocotyl* (the future adult stem), and *radicle* (root). That's a lot to pack in! As the seed first develops, the cotyledon contains all the food the baby plant needs to push up through the soil. Once the cotyledon is gone (about two weeks), the young plant begins to make its own food through photosynthesis.

1 **Give fruits and veggies** a good look and think about where their seeds are. Some are obvious (you can see the seeds inside a tomato, for example), while some are sneakier—a strawberry's little yellow dots are actually seeds! Extract these tiny packets of genetic info, rinse them off, and pat them dry.

2 **Arrange your harvested seeds** on a damp paper towel on top of a cookie sheet, categorizing them by type. Next, add some snack seeds and beans, too. (Got dried beans? Let them soak overnight in water first.)

3 **With a handheld magnifying glass,** look at your collection for similarities and differences. What colors, shapes, and textures do you see? What traits might protect the precious genetic data inside from predators?

4 **Now that you've studied** your seeds' outsides, it's time to investigate their guts! Pick one of each type to donate to science. With a small paring knife, cut into each seed. Explore the covering and the "meat" inside.

5 **Seeds are for growing,** so place your tray someplace safe and give it a daily spritz of water. Observe and record the growth of leaves and roots. Soon, you can transfer the seeds to soil and grow your own plants!

Seed coat

Epicotyl

Plumule

Cotyledon

Hypocotyl

Radicle

1. **Punch a nail** through a square of cardboard and carefully stick a shelled peanut on the nail's tip. Tape the cardboard to a table so the peanut is in the air.

2. **Next, make a stand.** Bend the triangular portion of a wire coat hanger into a base and tape it near the cardboard square so that the hooked end is over the peanut. Place a soda can on the hanger's hook so it's right above your test subject.

3. **Measure 100 mL of water.** Pour it into the can and use a candy thermometer to take its temperature. Jot it down.

4. **Ask your grown-up** to light the peanut on fire. Stand back—it's about to get hot in here! Watch the flame catch, blaze, and then slowly peter out, leaving a blackened nut.

5. **Grab your thermometer** and take the temperature of the water in the can again. You should see a spike in heat.

6. **Time for math.** It takes 1 calorie to raise 1 mL of water by 1 degree Celsius. Since your burning peanut changed the temperature of 100 mL of water, multiply the change in temperature (in degrees Celsius) by 100 to calculate how many calories are in your peanut. For example, if the water changed 30°C, your peanut released 3,000 calories!

What's the Deal?

All food has energy—that's why our bodies need it! When you burned the peanut, energy flowed from the snack via *combustion*, converting its hidden chemical energy into heat. When you eat a peanut, your body does the same thing: It converts the energy stored in the peanut into the energy it needs to keep running. For health purposes, the nutritional information on all food packaging reports how many calories a food contains. Since 1 food Calorie contains 1,000 calories, your peanut has 3 total food Calories. You can try this same experiment with other nuts—or even cheese puffs!—to see how they measure up. A lot of the peanut's energy ends up heating the surrounding air instead of the water, so the caloric estimate may be lower than what's on the package.

How Many Calories Are in a Peanut?

The best way to find out is to burn it to a crisp!

You'll need:

Small square of cardboard
Nail
Tape
Shelled peanut*
Wire coat hanger
Soda can
Water
Candy thermometer
Paper and pencil
Matches

*Extreme caution: No one with nut allergies should do this activity. Check with a grown-up first.

You'll need:

5 alligator-clip leads
Red LED
4 kosher dill pickles
Paring knife
4 copper coins
4 #6 or #8 galvanized nails

Pickle Power

Salty, snappy, a sandwich's best friend—and a source of hidden superpower!

What's the Deal?

Pickles contain saltwater, which is rich in *ions*—charged particles. Chemical reactions occur with the copper coin and zinc nail that start an electrical tug of war. A reaction at the nail produces electrons, and a reaction at the copper uses them. That sets electrons flowing in a current around the circuit, powering the LED. Ordinary batteries work the same way, minus the dill: They use two metals in ion-rich liquid to separate electrical charge and thus create a current. (But they taste lousy with pastrami on rye.)

1 *At a hobbyist shop,* buy five alligator-clip leads and a red LED.

2 *Back at home,* fork a pickle out of the jar. Cut a slit in it with a paring knife and insert a copper coin. Close to the copper coin, stick a #6 or #8 galvanized nail into the pickle. Do this with three more pickles.

3 *With an alligator-clip lead,* connect the nail in one pickle to the coin in a second pickle. Connect the nail in the second pickle to the coin in the third. Use a third lead to connect the nail in the third pickle to the coin in the fourth pickle.

4 *Like it bright, you say?* Now that your pickles are connected, use a lead to connect the coin in pickle #1 to the long leg of the LED. Use that last lead to connect the nail in #4 to the short leg. You should see the light blink on!

Try This Next!

Now that you've cooked up a basic circuit, take another look at your fruit basket and veggie bin: What other foodstuffs can you find to run low-power gadgets around the house? Try hooking a small, AA-powered clock face to a few unsuspecting lemons.

Salt

This dinner-table staple also goes by NaCl, a chemical compound of the elements sodium and chloride. When these two team up, big taste happens. But our bodies also need salt for proper nerve and muscle function, to maintain blood pressure, and to absorb nutrients in our intestines. We likely rely on it because we evolved with so much of it around us—and in such surprising forms.

Fresh water is a must for many creatures on Earth. But what do animals who spend most of their time near the salty ocean do? They evolve *salt glands*—specialized systems that excrete excess salt through their nostrils. If you ever see a sea bird appear to sneeze, it's probably getting rid of salt!

Salt glands

Preservative

Salt in its natural state is called *halite*. It formed when ancient seas evaporated millions of years ago, leaving the mineral behind in cube-shaped crystals. Next time you're at dinner, look closely and you'll see that table salt is made of tiny cubes, too. That's because crystals build themselves with the same infinitely repeating shapes. You can make your own salt crystals by letting a string sit in a supersaturated solution of water and salt for a few days.

Halite

One of salt's great uses is as a *preservative*. Via a chemical process called *osmosis*, salt absorbs water content from food items, which makes them too dry for harmful bacteria or mold to move in and start spoiling everything. We discovered salt's preservation superpower thousands of years ago, and it's led to the creation of some of our favorite foods: pickles, bacon, pastrami, and beef jerky!

Bolivia's Salar de Uyuni is the world's largest salt flat—it covers a massive 4,086 square miles (10,582 sq km)! Incredibly flat and bright white, the salt-crust surface of the salar shines like a huge mirror when it's covered in a thin layer of water—so much so that scientists use it to calibrate satellites in space.

Fleur de sel

The people of Guérande and Île de Ré, France, have harvested salt the same way for hundreds of years. Irrigation systems along the coast flood low-lying ponds with saltwater. The saltwater evaporates, leaving coarse crystals that the salt harvesters then rake up by hand. Some of the most valuable salt in the world is gathered this way—it's called *fleur de sel*.

Salar de Uyuni

Salty sweetness

Salt is one of the tastes humans know—and like!—best. But did you know it makes sweet stuff taste sweeter? Scientists aren't sure why this happens; some believe that salt disrupts our taste buds, making them suppress bitterness. Others think the confusion happens in our brains, not our mouths. Next time you have ice cream, try a little salt as a topping!

Great Icescapes

Turn a globe of ice into an artistic wonder.

1. **A few days in advance,** ready your ice balloons. Fill two balloons with water until they're about 5 inches (13 cm) in diameter. Place them in the freezer.

2. **When the ice balloons** are frozen, use scissors to cut off their knots. Then peel the balloons off the ice, and place them in your tub. Give them a close look. Turn on your flashlight to illuminate those chilly spheres, and peer at the details with a magnifying lens. Do you see spikes, cracks, or frost?

3. **Poke at the ice** with toothpicks and unfolded paper clips. Which is more effective at getting into the ice, the wood or the metal?

4. **Pour a little salt** on the ice. It should begin to eat into the surface, which will melt into beautiful ridges and tunnels.

5. **Now drizzle food coloring** on the ice. Start with one color and notice how it spreads and highlights parts of the ice ball, and then go crazy and add as many colors as you want. Some will remain on the ice's surface, while others will seep down into the cracks made by the salt!

What's the Deal?
When ice freezes, air gets stuck inside, creating whiskery "spikes" of trapped air. Internal pressure as the water freezes causes the cracks you observed, while the frost is made of ice crystals that form on the ice ball's surface. The paper clips and toothpicks affect the ice differently because of their *thermal conductivity*: The metal melts the ice more quickly than the wood because it's better at channeling heat. Salt also melts the ice by lowering its *melting point* (the temperature at which a solid changes to a liquid), which is why it's used to de-ice snowy roads in the winter.

Incredible
Salt-sational Lava Lamps

Who knew basic cooking ingredients could be so hypnotizing?

You'll need:

Water
Clear jar or bottle with a lid
⅓ cup (80 mL) vegetable oil
Food coloring
Salt
Glitter

What's the Deal?

Pause and think about things that you've seen float and sink. Objects that are light bob merrily on the surface, while things that are heavy plummet to the bottom. The same principle is at work here: Oil floats at the top of the bottle because it's less dense than water. Plus, oil and water are *immiscible liquids*, which means they refuse to mix! But when you pour salt in the bottle, it sinks to the bottom (because the salt is denser than water) and it carries a blob of oil with it. Then, in a surprise twist, the salt dissolves in the water, meaning that its sodium and chloride molecules drift apart. When the salt dissolves, the blob of oil is released and floats back to the surface, bubbling and rolling. The glitter behaves similarly to the salt, only it doesn't dissolve. Instead, it collects into a floating glitter globe, resulting in a permanently extracool *glug-a-glug* effect.

1 Pour about 3 inches (7.5 cm) of water into a clear jar or bottle. (You may want to use more than one container so you can experiment with different ratios, as shown here.)

2 Pour ⅓ cup (80 mL) of vegetable oil into the bottle. Watch the liquids as they settle. Look closely: Does the oil sink or float on top of the water? Try shaking it up. Do you see any difference in the way the liquids interact?

3 Add one drop of food coloring to the bottle and watch where it goes. Does the drop naturally gravitate toward mixing with the oil or with the water? Does the color spread in the liquids?

4 Sprinkle salt on top of the oil at the top of the jar while you count slowly to five. Wow! What happens to the food coloring? What happens to the salt? Add more salt to keep the action going for as long as you want.

5 Put in some glitter, and then put the lid on the bottle and give it a good shake. How does the glitter behave differently from the salt?

Why is sourdough bread so light and fluffy? It hosts a microbial monster that gobbles up sugar!

Start Some Sourdough

1 **Make a mound** of ⅓ cup (45 g) of flour on a clean counter. Create a well in the center and add 1 or 2 tablespoons of warm water. Mix the flour and water slowly, swirling more flour from the edges into the center of the well as you go. The mixture will gradually start to look like a small piece of dough. Here's your sourdough "starter"—aka yeast trap!

2 **Knead this piece of dough** until it becomes springy, about 5 to 8 minutes. Place it in a bowl, cover with a damp towel, and let it sit in a warm spot, about 70°F (21°C), for 2 or 3 days. (Leave it longer if your room is cool.) When it's ready, the dough will be moist, wrinkled, and crusty. Pull off some crust—you'll see tiny bubbles and smell a sweet aroma. That's a sure sign of *fermentation*—the process by which sugar gets converted into carbon dioxide, making your bread rise.

3 **Pick off any hardened crust** and toss it. Now it's time to "feed" your yeast: Add ⅔ cup (85 g) of flour and enough water to make a firm dough. Set the bowl aside, covered and in a warm place, for another 1 or 2 days.

4 **When the starter** starts to look moist and wrinkled again, it's time for another feeding. (Hey, a growing starter needs its lunch!) Remove any crusty bits and mix the rest with 1 cup (125 g) of flour. Put the starter in its covered bowl in a warm place for 8 to 12 hours.

5 **To test it for doneness,** try poking the starter gently with your finger: If it doesn't spring back, it's ready to star in the creation of a fresh loaf of sourdough.

Turn the page ⟹

What's the Deal?

Yeast is a single-celled fungus that exists all around us. And when you made a tempting, warm mixture of flour and water, yeast found a great place to grow and moved right in! Your dough contains not only flour, water, and yeast, but lactic acid bacteria that feeds on the sugar in the flour. This bacteria gives sourdough its signature tangy taste. But if all breads contain bacteria, how come not all breads are sour? In dough made with store-bought baker's yeast, the yeast outnumber the bacteria, so they don't have a chance to produce acid—and that tangy flavor. But *Saccharomyces exiguus*, the yeast in sourdough, cannot consume *maltose*, one of the sugars in flour. The result is that sourdough's bacteria don't have to compete with the yeast for food, and so they thrive and deliver that acidic zing to your tongue. Meanwhile, the yeast in store-bought starters gobbles maltose right up, depriving the bacteria of a food source—and the bread of that distinct taste!

6 **Take a piece** of starter the size of a tangerine, dilute it in warm water, and then mix in 2 cups (250 g) of flour. (Don't use all your starter in one go! Store some in the fridge for future bread-baking.) Cover this mixture and set it in a warm spot for 18 to 24 hours, until it's bubbly. You're waking up the yeast here—you'll want it lively!

7 **Mix the remaining flour** (about ½ cup/65 g) and the salt together in a separate bowl. Pour ¾ cup of your starter in and mix the ingredients. Then, slowly add cool water and mix until it forms a ball.

8 **Place the mixture** on a well-floured work table and round it into a ball. Put the dough in a well-oiled, covered bowl and let it rise in the fridge for 12 to 15 hours. Remove and allow it to warm up at room temperature for 2 hours.

9 **Divide the dough** into two pieces, and stretch them into baguette shapes. Place each one on a parchment-lined baking tray.

10 **Cover the baguettes** with the towel. Let them rise for 6 to 7 hours, until they have doubled in size. With each rise, the yeast eats up sugar and releases carbon dioxide, making the dough expand.

11 **Preheat the oven** to 450°F (232°C). Using a kitchen knife, slash the loaves' tops and spray with a fine mist of water.

12 **Place the loaves in the oven.** Spray them, as well as the walls of the oven, with water. Repeat after 5 minutes.

13 **Bake the loaves** 25 to 30 minutes, until they are entirely golden.

What's the Deal?

There's lots of sweet science at work in these meringues! Egg whites foam because they contain proteins, and beating them makes their building blocks, called *amino acids*, uncurl. Some amino acids are *hydrophilic* (they love to bond with water) while some are *hydrophobic* (they stay away from H_2O). The hydrophobic ones are pushed to the surface and merge with the air bubbles that you introduce by whisking, creating airiness. When you mix in vinegar (an acid), its positively charged hydrogen ions get in the way of proteins bonding tightly to each other. They stay bound loosely to air bubbles, which get packed into the meringue. In the oven, the sugar strengthens the bonds between the proteins and helps the meringue hold, baking that frothiness into mini melt-in-your-mouth clouds!

1 Preheat the oven to 250°F (121°C). Crack open a room-temperature egg in a small, shallow dish. Scoop it up so that the yolk rests in your hand and the goopy white drips off. Repeat with three more eggs, putting the egg whites into a metal bowl. (Save the yolks for another dish!) Add the white vinegar and beat until the egg whites get big and fluffy.

2 Once the egg whites have transformed into a heap of airy foaminess, slowly add the sugar a little at a time, whisking as you go. Keep whisking for at least 5 minutes after all the sugar is in the mix.

3 The egg whites are ready when you can pull your whisk out of the whites and they stay standing up in little waves, which bakers call *soft peaks*. Add the cornstarch and vanilla and whisk thoroughly.

4 Line a baking sheet with parchment paper and spoon little heaps of egg white onto it. Bake for 20 to 25 minutes, and then turn the oven off and let it cool with the door ajar. Now you've got meringues—delicious desserts made strong by egg proteins!

2. Whisking makes them *denature*, or uncurl, introducing air bubbles.

1. Tightly coiled proteins are hanging out in the egg whites.

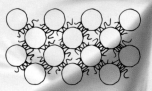

3. The amino acid chains that make up the proteins bond with the air bubbles to form a frothy, foamy network.

These desserts may look delicate, but the egg whites inside are superstrong.

Mighty Meringues

You'll need:

Small, shallow dish
4 egg whites*
Glass or metal bowl (no plastic!)
½ teaspoon white vinegar
Whisk or egg beater
⅔ cup (130 g) sugar
Cream of tartar or cornstarch
1 teaspoon vanilla extract
Baking sheet
Parchment paper

*Don't let any yolk get into the bowl!

Exploding Marshmallows!

Zap a marshmallow to make a behemoth—
and learn what microwaves do to sugar
molecules while you're at it.

1. **Place two marshmallows** on a microwave-safe plate or paper towel, then put them in the microwave. Nuke on high for 1 minute.

2. **Watch through the window** of the microwave. After 20 seconds, you'll see the marshmallows puff up—they'll grow to about four times their original size! When the minute is up, take the plate out and let the treats cool.

3. **Pick a marshmallow** for a thorough investigation. Is it hollow inside? Is the inside the same color as the outside? When you eat it, is it soft or crunchy? Let the other marshmallow sit, and observe as it shrinks into a gooey heap, which you can pull apart.

4. **Make mallows joust!** Place two chick- or bunny-shaped marshmallows across from each other on a paper towel and push wooden toothpicks into them. Nuke them for 1 minute and watch the jousting through the window!

What's the Deal?

Marshmallows are mostly sugar and water wrapped around a bunch of air bubbles, which is why they're so wonderfully light. When you cook them in a microwave, the water molecules inside vibrate very quickly—which in turn makes the water heat up and warms the sugar, rendering it soft and gooey. The air molecules get heated up too, pushing harder against the air-bubble walls. These bubbles expand and the marshmallow puffs up so it's big. But if it pumps up too much, some bubbles burst, deflating the mallow like a popped balloon. Once it cools, the bubbles shrink and the sugar hardens. Now it's dry and crunchy—likely because the water inside evaporated when it got hot. Cook it longer and the marshmallow turns brown. That's a process called caramelization, one of the fundamentals of cooking.

Try This Next!

How do microwave ovens work? They use *electromagnetic waves*, vibrating energy that we harness to heat up food really fast. You can't see these waves with the naked eye. But if you remove your microwave's turntable and nuke a marshmallow-lined dish on low for a few minutes, you'll start to see a pattern: Some marshmallow sections will look more melted or puffier than others. (The exact effect depends on your microwave model.) Those are standing electromagnetic waves at work!

Sugar

This deliciously sweet substance is much more than an ingredient in our favorite tasty treats—it's what fuels our bodies for all the events of the day! Made up of carbon, hydrogen, and oxygen atoms, sugar molecules team up into *carbohydrates*, the main source of energy for lots of living creatures. Here's the scoop on the sweet stuff.

Scientists have found *glycolaldehyde*—a simple sugar molecule—in a cloud of gas where stars are born in the Milky Way galaxy. This molecule can combine with others to create *ribose* (a building block of our genes) and *glucose* (the most abundant simple sugar in living organisms). Glycolaldehyde's existence in this cloud could mean that it was present when our planet first formed—and could have helped give rise to life.

Sugar in space

Sugar in nature

All plant tissues contain sugar, but the tiny white crystals that you buy at the store—known as *sucrose*—come from sugarcane or sugar beets. That's because sugar is highly concentrated in these plants, so it's easy to crush them and squeeze out the sweet gooey stuff inside (a process called *extraction*). Humans have also long satisfied their sugar cravings with honey from bees and syrup from trees.

In the movies, people crash through windows all the time—sometimes that glass is made of sugar! Bring 2 cups (470 mL) of water, 1 cup (235 mL) of corn syrup, 3½ cups (700 g) of sugar, and ¼ teaspoon of cream of tartar to a boil very slowly. Let the mix reach 260°F (126°C) and pour it onto a greased cookie sheet. Let it cool, pry it loose, and keep it in the fridge until you're ready to use it—and then let the comedy begin. (Careful, this "glass" can be sharp.)

Sugar glass

It's obvious that some foods and drinks have a ton (we're looking at you, soda and candy), but some unlikely suspects are full of the sweet stuff, too. For instance, 1 tablespoon of some ketchup brands contains up to 1 teaspoon of sugar, and lots of frozen foods pack sugar in as a preservative that helps them taste fresh. And surprisingly, many foods containing fruit, which is already sweet, have a lot of added sugar. Fruit juice, for instance, may have as much as 7 teaspoons of sugar per 8 ounces (236 mL)! So make sure you read the labels before you snack.

Secret sugar

There's a rainbow of sugar colors and textures out there! The most common is *granulated sugar* (or *sucrose*). It gets its snow-white color and fine cubes in a process called *refining*, which removes molasses from the sugarcane or beet and helps crystals start to form. There's also confectioners' sugar—a fluffy powder that's been ground down finely for use in icing and other treats—and brown sugar, which is refined sugar with the molasses left in for an extra-syrupy taste! What other kinds do you know?

Sugar and health

Just because it tastes good doesn't mean it's good for you! Sugar lacks nutrients, minerals, or proteins—so it offers no real benefits besides energy. Eating too much sugar is linked to problems like diabetes— in which the body doesn't create enough insulin (a crucial substance that helps cells get glucose from food)—and cavities. When you eat something sweet, the bacteria in your mouth feast on the sugar stuck to your teeth. They then create acids that eat your teeth's enamel. So you'd better brush! And it's a good idea to avoid drinking or eating lots of sugar to begin with.

Stretchable Edible Science

What makes some sugary candies rock hard and others soft and chewy? Air bubbles—and your mighty muscles.

You'll need:

2 cups (400 g) sugar
2 tablespoons cornstarch
Saucepan
1 cup (235 mL) light corn syrup
2 teaspoons glycerin
¾ cup (180 mL) water
2 tablespoons butter
1 teaspoon salt
Pastry brush
Candy thermometer
3 drops food coloring
¼ to 1 teaspoon flavoring
Greased cookie sheet
Waxed paper

1 Mix together the sugar and cornstarch in the saucepan. Stir in the corn syrup, glycerin, water, butter, and salt. Place the saucepan over medium heat, stirring until the sugar dissolves.

2 Keep stirring until the mixture begins to boil, and then let it cook undisturbed. At this point, you have dissolved the crystal structure of the sugar—which is just what you want! But be careful: Any agitation from here on out can encourage the fructose and glucose molecules in your syrup to rejoin and form sucrose crystals, aka taffy's mortal enemy!

3 As the syrup cooks, continually wash down the pan's sides with a pastry brush dipped in warm water. This keeps tiny sugar crystals out of the mix.

4 Boil the mixture until the candy thermometer reads 270°F (132°C), which is called the *soft-crack stage*. The bubbles on top will become smaller, thicker, and closer together. Try dropping a bit of this syrup into cold water. You'll see it solidify into threads that are flexible but not brittle.

5 Remove the saucepan from the heat and add your food coloring and flavoring. Stir gently and then pour onto a greased cookie sheet to cool.

6 Let the candy cool enough so you can touch it. Now for the fun—stretching and bending that delicious soon-to-be taffy! This step, of course, is

What's the Deal?

When you walk into a candy store, hundreds of treats seem to be calling your name. So you may be surprised to learn that there are really only two types of candy: *crystalline* candies such as fudge, which get their smooth texture from fine sucrose (sugar) crystals, and *noncrystalline* delights, such as taffy or hard candies, in which the sugar is dissolved throughout. Taffy requires a nonsucrose sugar, such as corn syrup (mainly glucose), to keep sugar molecules from locking together into crystals. But what's with all the pulling? It's not just exercise: Pulling the taffy aerates the sugar, incorporating tiny air bubbles throughout and making it even lighter and chewier.

better done with a friend. Grease your hands with oil or butter and pull the taffy, stretching it out, folding it in half, and repeating this for 10 minutes. You want the taffy to end up light in color with a satiny gloss.

7 Roll the pulled taffy into a long rope, about ½ inch (1.25 cm) in diameter. You can cut it with a buttered knife into 1-inch- (2.5-cm-) long pieces, or you could braid strands or make pinwheels or twists. Let the pieces sit for half an hour, and then wrap each one in waxed paper.

No-Apple Apple Pie

Flavors can be deceiving—sometimes you don't need a key ingredient to get the taste you're after!

You'll need:

Pie crust dough, enough for a double-crust, 9-inch (23-cm) pie

9-inch (23-cm) pie tin

1¾ cups (240 g) buttery snack crackers (such as Ritz), crushed up in a zipper-locked bag

1¾ cups (415 mL) water

2 cups (400 g) sugar

2 teaspoons cream of tartar

Pot

2 tablespoons lemon juice

Zest of 1 lemon

2 tablespoons butter

½ teaspoon ground cinnamon

String

Scissors

1 **Divide the pie crust dough** in half and roll out one half to line a pie tin. Sprinkle the crushed-up crackers evenly into the lined pie tin.

2 **Next, make a syrup** to pour over this unlikely crust filling! Put the water, sugar, and cream of tartar into a pot and bring it to a boil on the stove. Then reduce the heat and let it simmer for 15 minutes. Take it off the heat and add the lemon juice and the zest. Once the syrup has cooled down, pour it evenly over the cracker pieces.

3 **Cut up the butter** into small cubes. Dot the pie filling with the butter and follow up with a hearty sprinkling of cinnamon.

4 **Roll out the other half** of the pie crust dough and cut it into long strips, each 1 inch (2.5 cm) wide. Assemble a lattice across the top, interweaving the strips so there's space for steam to escape. Trim any strips hanging over the pie edge.

What's the Deal?

If there are no apples in this pie, why is the flavor so surprisingly similar to that of apple pie? Because we taste and smell specific molecules, not specific foods. Food scientists know how to synthesize the odor and taste molecules of many common foods, making it possible to mimic real flavor with artificial flavor. Mock apple pie didn't come from a lab, though. It was invented as a substitute during World War II when apples were scarce and expensive. Have you ever tasted an ingredient that reminded you of something else? Try it as a substitute in your next recipe.

5 **Bake at 425°F** (218°C) for 30 to 35 minutes. Let it cool, then cut a slice for an unsuspecting family member to taste-test. Do their taste buds scream "Apple pie!"—or can they make out the cracker impostor?

Try This Next!

Pie isn't just for eating! Pi, represented by the Greek letter π, is a mathematical constant consisting of the ratio of a circle's *diameter* (the distance across it) to its *circumference* (the distance around it). To enjoy this never-ending, never-repeating number, wrap a string around your pie tin, and then cut the string to that distance. Stretch the string across the top of the pie, doubling back across until you're out of string. You'll see three complete diameters, plus a bit left over, because π = 3.14159 . . .

1. **Using wire cutters,** cut and then wrap wires around the LED's positive and negative leads. The wire attached to the longer (positive) LED leg should be longer than the wire attached to the shorter (negative) leg. Cover the connections with electrical tape to protect them from the solution.

2. **Heat the water** in the pot, and then add 1 cup (200 g) of sugar at a time as it heats. Stir and let it dissolve. After it cools, pour the syrup into paper cups, filling them about ½ inch (1.25 cm) away from the rim.

3. **Roll the LED heads** in loose sugar. This "seeds" the LEDs with sugar crystals, which will create more crystals when you soak the LEDs in the sugar solution.

4. **Wrap the wires** on the LEDs around individual skewers or pencils. Place them over the cups so the LEDs are submerged in the solution.

5. **Wait two weeks,** and then gingerly peel away the paper cups and break loose the crystals inside.

6. **Let the crystals** dry for a day. Slide a 3-volt battery between an LED's wires to light it up. The positive side of the battery should touch the LED's longer leg. Tape and find brilliant uses for all your sweet bling.

What's the Deal?

When you add the sugar to the water, you create a *saturated solution*, a mixure in which the sugar dissolves as much as possible without settling at the bottom. When you heat it and let it cool, you change it to a *supersaturated solution*, since some of the water evaporates. This results in sugar coming out of the solution, forming a *precipitate*. As days pass, the water in the paper cup evaporates more, and the precipitate sugar collects on the seed crystals on the LED. An uncountable number of molecules will make up your finished rock candy. They'll cause the LED's light to glow and spread throughout the candy. Now that's a bright idea!

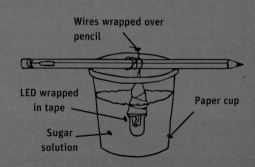

Wires wrapped over pencil

LED wrapped in tape

Paper cup

Sugar solution

Blinging Candy Crystals

Rock candy shows you the shape of sugar crystals on a giant scale. Bonus: These also glow.

You'll need:

Wire cutters
Electrical wire
LEDs in different colors
Electrical tape
2 cups (470 mL) water
Pot
4 cups (800 g) sugar
Paper cups
Skewers or pencils
3-volt coin batteries

Index

Index

Activity Credits

Thanks to all the Exploratorium staff and participants of the Teacher Institute, Institute for Inquiry, Extended Learning, and Community Youth Programs, who contributed to the creation, testing, and continued development of these activities. In particular, certain activities couldn't have happened without Eric Muller and Julie Yu.

Special thanks to Emily Daniels for developing the rock candy rings on page 104.

Weldon Owen Acknowledgments

Weldon Owen would like to thank the Exploratorium for blowing our minds with science throughout the creation of this book. Special thanks go to rock-star educators Ken Finn, Eric Muller, Linda Shore, and Julie Yu for their invaluable help in evaluating the activities. We'd also like to thank Julie Nunn, Silva Raker, Dana Goldberg, Ruth Brown, and Amy Snyder for their enthusiasm, expertise, and assistance. The Exploratorium also gratefully acknowledges its Catalyst Circle Committee for its leadership in resource development, which advances the museum's educational mission.

We'd also like to express gratitude to our photo shoot team: our photograher, Katrine Naleid; Stephen Austin Welch; Victor Wong; stylist Pamela Campbell; assistant stylist Hilary Seeley; food stylist Victoria Woolard; and studio teachers Carolyn Crimley, Bonnie Hughes, and Nancy Riordan. We'd also like to thank Elissa Worley at Exalt Models and all our amazing kid scientists on set: Annalie, Brian, Cruz, Emily, Faith, Gianna, Giovanni, Isabella, Jonathan, Kaylyn, Mariah, Matthew, Sydney, and Taylor.

We also must give a hearty thanks to Kevin Broccoli, Sarah Edelstein, Laura Harger, Lisa Marietta, Gail Nelson-Bonebrake, and Molly Stewart for editorial assistance, and Andreina Prado and Hilary Seeley for design help.

weldon**owen**

President, Publisher Roger Shaw
Senior VP, Sales Amy Kaneko
Director of Finance Philip Paulick

Senior Editor Lucie Parker
Project Editor Emily Wolahan
Editorial Assistant Jaime Alfaro

Creative Director Kelly Booth
Art Director Lorraine Rath
Project Art Director Meghan Hildebrand
Senior Production Designer Rachel Lopez Metzger

Production Director Chris Hemesath
Associate Production Director Michelle Duggan

Weldon Owen is a division of **BONNIER**

Library of Congress Control Number: 2014955784

ISBN 13: 978-1-61628-800-6
ISBN 10: 1-61628-800-0

10 9 8 7 6 5 4 3 2 1
2015 2016 2017 2018

Printed and bound in China.

expl◯ratorium®

Pier 15, San Francisco, CA 94111
www.exploratorium.edu

The Exploratorium is San Francisco's renowned museum of
science, art, and human perception. The content in this book
began as exhibitions, workshops, and activities created through
the Exploratorium's educational and professional development
programs. These long-standing, highly regarded programs include
the Teacher Institute, which supports secondary science and
math teachers; the Institute for Inquiry, which offers workshops
about the theory and practice of inquiry; and the Community
Youth Program, which provides programs for children, youth, and
families in partnership with community organizations. For more
information, visit www.exploratorium.edu.

Exploratorium® is a registered trademark and service mark of
the Exploratorium.

Image Credits

All cover photographs by Katrine Naleid.

All interior photography by Katrine Naleid unless noted below.

Thomas Deerinck, NCMIR/Science Source: 91 Laura Hamilton; 39
(capillary action) Inmagine: 28–29 (all except noni) Erin Kunkel:
23, 34 Ian Monty: 84 (Solar de Uyuni) NASA: 98 (sugar in space)
Orbital Joe: 84 (halite) Shutterstock: 10–11, 13, 14, 17, 20, 21, 28
(noni), 32, 38 (states of matter, water from space), 39 (heat
capacity, universal solvent), 52–53, 64–65, 84 (preservative, salt
glands), 85 (fleur de sel, salty sweetness), 94, 98 (sugar in nature,
sugar glass), 99 (sugar types, sugar and health, secret sugar),
108–109, 110, 112 Amy Snyder (© Exploratorium): 8–9
Wikicommons (user Alvesgaspar): 38 (surface tension)

Illustrations by Lorraine Rath and Jenna Rosenthal.